Preface

The increasing reliance on digital platforms Security and Cyber Laws Digital Defenders has brought significant advancements in communication, business, and daily life. However, with this rapid technological growth comes a heightened risk of cyber threats and legal challenges. As cybercrime continues to evolve, the demand for professionals well-versed in cybersecurity and cyber laws is greater than ever. This book, *Security and Cyber Laws: Digital Defenders*, has been meticulously designed to provide a comprehensive understanding of cybersecurity concepts, best practices, and the legal framework governing digital security.

Purpose and Scope

This book aims to serve as a complete guide for students, educators, and professionals interested in the domains of cybersecurity and cyber law. Covering fundamental principles, emerging threats, and legal regulations, it offers a structured approach to understanding both the technical and legal aspects of digital security. The content is aligned with academic curricula, ensuring readers are well-prepared for exams, certifications, and professional challenges in the field of cybersecurity.

Unique Features of the Book

We believe that an effective learning experience combines theoretical knowledge with practical applications. To meet this goal, the book includes the following unique features:

Comprehensive Theory with Clear Explanations:

Each chapter explains key cybersecurity and legal concepts in a detailed manner, supported by real-world examples, diagrams, and case studies to facilitate better understanding.

Diverse Exercises:

To reinforce the knowledge gained, a variety of exercises are included:

Multiple Choice Questions (MCQs): Test conceptual clarity and prepare for competitive exams.

True/False: Strengthen factual understanding and help in quick revision.

Match the Case: Develop critical thinking by understanding relationships between various cybersecurity concepts.

Jumbled Words and Rearranging Sentences: Enhance vocabulary and comprehension of technical terms related to cybersecurity.

Interactive Content and Videos:

Recognizing the importance of multimedia learning, we have supplemented the book with QR codes linked to videos. These videos explain complex topics in an engaging way, helping learners grasp difficult concepts more effectively.

Test Papers and Sample Papers:

A range of test papers, sample papers, and previous years' question papers are included to help readers practice thoroughly. These are designed to enhance problem-solving skills and improve time management during exams.

Viva Voce Questions:

A section dedicated to frequently asked viva voce questions is provided, covering both basic and advanced topics to help students prepare effectively for oral examinations.

This book is ideal for:

Undergraduate and postgraduate students pursuing courses in cybersecurity, information technology, and legal studies.

Professionals seeking to enhance their understanding of cyber laws and digital security practices.

Educators and trainers looking for a resourceful guide to aid in teaching cybersecurity and cyber law.

Acknowledgments

We extend our heartfelt gratitude to the subject matter experts, legal professionals, and cybersecurity specialists who provided invaluable guidance and feedback during the development of this book. We also thank our editorial and design teams for their dedication in making this a truly interactive and user-friendly learning resource.

AF518504

Table of Contents

Chapter 1 - Introduction to Cyber Security

In this Chapter you will learn about:

Cyberspace and the Internet of Things
Cyber Security Threats
Cyber Crimes
Cyber Laws
Cyber Criminals
Law Enforcement Roles and Responses

Cyberlaw governs the legal aspects of the internet and digital technologies, addressing issues like Online privacy, Data protection, and Cybercrime. As the internet facilitates global communication and commerce, it also introduces risks such as hacking and fraud. Cyberlaw provides the framework to protect individuals, businesses, and governments in this digital era, ensuring online activities' security and enforcing legal rights in cyberspace. It also adapts to emerging technologies like artificial intelligence and the Internet of Things (IoT), offering guidelines for their ethical and legal use.

1.1 Cyberspace and the Internet of Things

Cyberspace

Cyberspace is a virtual environment where digital communications and transactions occur. It encompasses the internet, computer networks, and all the digital Data they transmit. People interact through social media, email, and various online platforms in cyberspace. It has revolutionised how we communicate, conduct business, and access information. However, this vast digital realm also presents challenges, such as cybercrime and the need for effective regulation, making understanding cyberspace crucial today.

The Internet of Things (IoT)

Refers to the network of physical devices, vehicles, appliances, and other objects embedded with sensors, software, and connectivity that allows them to collect and exchange Data over the internet. IoT devices range from smart home gadgets like thermostats and security cameras to industrial machines and healthcare devices. The IoT has the potential to transform industries by increasing efficiency, improving services, and enabling innovations. However, the proliferation of IoT devices also raises significant cybersecurity and privacy concerns, as these interconnected systems can be vulnerable to hacking and Data breaches.

1.2 Cyber Crimes

Phishing Attacks

Phishing is a deceptive technique cybercriminals use to trick individuals into revealing sensitive information, such as passwords and credit card numbers. Attackers often masquerade as trustworthy entities through fake emails or websites. Victims are lured into clicking malicious links, leading to Data breaches and Financial losses.

Ransomware

Ransomware is malicious software that encrypts a victim's Data, rendering it inaccessible. The attacker then demands a ransom in exchange for the decryption key. These attacks can cripple businesses and individuals alike, causing significant financial and operational damage.

Identity Theft

Identity theft involves stealing someone's personal information, like social security numbers or credit card details, to commit fraud. Cybercriminals use this information to impersonate victims, making unauthorised transactions or opening accounts in their names, leading to financial loss and damaged credit.

Denial-of-Service (DoS) Attacks

A Denial-of-Service attack overwhelms a network or website with excessive traffic, rendering it unavailable to legitimate users. This type of attack disrupts the normal functioning of services, often leading to significant downtime and financial losses for businesses.

1.3 Cyber Criminals

Phishing Attacks

Cybercriminals use phishing to deceive individuals into providing sensitive information, such as passwords or credit card numbers. These attacks often involve fake emails or websites that appear legitimate but are designed to steal personal Data. Phishing is one of the most common and effective techniques cybercriminals use today.

Ransomware

Ransomware is a type of malware that encrypts the victim's Data, making it inaccessible until a ransom is paid. Cybercriminals typically demand payment in cryptocurrency, making it difficult to trace. Ransomware attacks have surged in recent years, targeting businesses, healthcare institutions, and even government agencies.

Identity Theft

Identity theft occurs when cybercriminals steal personal information, such as Social Security numbers or bank account details, to commit fraud. They may use this information to open new accounts, make purchases, or even take out loans in the victim's name. Identity theft can have long-lasting effects on an individual's financial stability and credit score.

Social Engineering

Social engineering involves manipulating people into divulging confidential information or performing actions compromising security. Cybercriminals often exploit human psychology, such as trust or fear, to trick victims into revealing passwords or installing malicious software. This technique bypasses traditional security measures by targeting the human element.

DDoS Attacks

Distributed Denial of Service (DDoS) attacks aim to overwhelm a target's online services, such as a website or server, by flooding it with traffic from multiple sources. Cybercriminals use DDoS attacks to disrupt businesses, extort money, or simply cause chaos. These attacks can be difficult to mitigate, resulting in significant downtime and financial loss.

1.4 Cyber Security Threats

Cyber security threats encompass various potential dangers to information systems, Data, and networks. These threats can come from multiple sources, including cybercriminals, nation-state actors, and even insiders within an organisation. Common cyber security threats include malware, phishing attacks, ransomware, and denial-of-service (DoS) attacks. These threats aim to steal sensitive information, disrupt operations, or cause financial damage. As technology evolves, so do the methods and sophistication of these threats, making robust cyber security measures essential for individuals and organisations alike.

Types of Cyber Security threats:

1. **Malware:** Malware is malicious software designed to harm or exploit any programmable device, service, or network. Common types include viruses, worms, trojans, and spyware. Malware can disrupt operations, steal sensitive information, or grant unauthorised access to systems.
2. **Phishing:** Phishing attacks involve cybercriminals impersonating legitimate entities to trick individuals into providing sensitive information, such as passwords or credit card details. These attacks often occur via email, fake websites, or social media.
3. **Ransomware:** Ransomware is a type of malware that encrypts a victim's Data, rendering it inaccessible until a ransom is paid. Cybercriminals typically demand payment in cryptocurrency to maintain anonymity, making it challenging to trace them.
4. **Denial of Service (DoS) and Distributed Denial of Service (DDoS) Attacks:** In a DoS attack, cybercriminals flood a system with traffic, overwhelming it and causing it to crash or become unavailable. A DDoS attack amplifies this by using multiple compromised systems to launch the attack, making it more difficult to mitigate.
5. **Man-in-the-Middle (MitM) Attacks:** In MitM attacks, cybercriminals intercept communication between two parties to steal or alter information. This can occur through compromised Wi-Fi networks, where attackers eavesdrop on or manipulate exchanged data.
6. **SQL Injection:** SQL injection attacks occur when cybercriminals exploit vulnerabilities in a website's Database by inserting malicious code into SQL queries. This can allow them to gain unauthorised access to Data, modify it, or even delete it entirely.

1.5 Cyber Laws

Cyber laws are the legal frameworks that govern activities conducted on the internet and in cyberspace. These laws are designed to protect individuals, organisations, and governments from cybercrimes such as hacking, identity theft, and Data breaches. Cyber laws cover a wide range of issues, including privacy, intellectual property, e-commerce, and the regulation of digital currencies. As technology evolves, so too do the laws that regulate it, making cyber laws a constantly developing area of legal practice. Cyber laws ensure digital technology's safe and secure use, protect users from cyber threats, and maintain order in the digital world.

Key Areas of Cyber Law

1. Data Protection and Privacy:

Overview: Laws governing personal data collection, storage, and use.

Examples: General Data Protection Regulation (GDPR) in the EU, California Consumer Privacy Act (CCPA) in the US.

Key Issues: Consent, Data breaches, rights of Data subjects.

2. Cybercrimes:

Overview: Crimes conducted via the Internet include hacking, phishing, identity theft, and cyberstalking.

Legal Provisions: Computer Fraud and Abuse Act (CFAA) in the US, Information Technology Act, 2000 in India.

Challenges: Cross-border jurisdiction, anonymity, rapid technological changes.

3. Intellectual Property (IP) in Cyberspace:

Overview: Protection of copyrights, trademarks, and patents online.

Digital Piracy: Illegal downloading and sharing of copyrighted materials.

Domain Name Disputes: Issues related to cybersquatting and trademark infringement.

4. E-Commerce and Digital Contracts:

Overview: Legal recognition of electronic contracts, digital signatures, and online transactions.

E-Signature Laws: Electronic Signatures in Global and National Commerce Act (E-SIGN Act) in the US.

Consumer Protection: Laws ensuring consumer rights in online transactions.

5. Cybersecurity Laws:

Overview: Regulations to protect systems, networks, and Data from cyber-attacks.

National and International Frameworks: Includes laws like the Cybersecurity Information Sharing Act (CISA) in the US and international norms set by the United Nations.

Critical Infrastructure: Legal requirements for protecting essential services like finance, healthcare, and energy.

6. International Perspectives on Cyber Law

Jurisdiction: Different laws across countries complicate legal enforcement in cross-border cybercrimes.

Harmonization Efforts: International treaties and agreements, such as the Budapest Convention on Cybercrime, aim to standardise cyber laws.

Role of International Organizations: The United Nations, International Telecommunication Union (ITU), and others contribute to shaping global cyber laws.

1.6 Law Enforcement Roles and Responses

Law enforcement agencies ensure public safety, enforce laws and maintain social order. They prevent and investigate crimes, respond to emergencies, manage public events, and control traffic, all while working to build trust within the communities they serve. Additionally, they play a vital role in national security by engaging in counterterrorism efforts and coordinating with other agencies to protect the public from potential threats. Their multifaceted responsibilities are central to upholding justice and the rule of law in society.

1. Crime Prevention

Law enforcement agencies are tasked with preventing crime before it occurs. This involves proactive strategies such as regular patrolling, where officers maintain a visible community presence to deter potential criminals. Community policing is another key strategy, emphasising the importance of building relationships with local residents to identify and address issues that could lead to criminal behaviour. Law enforcement can gather valuable information, enhance trust, and work collaboratively to create safer neighbourhoods by engaging with the community. Additionally, crime awareness programs educate the public on safety measures, helping individuals and businesses protect themselves from becoming victims of crime.

2. Crime Investigation

When a crime occurs, law enforcement agencies are responsible for investigating the incident to identify and apprehend the perpetrator. This process includes collecting and analysing evidence, often using forensic techniques such as DNA analysis, fingerprinting, and digital forensics. Surveillance and the questioning of witnesses and suspects are also crucial components of crime investigation. Law enforcement officers must meticulously gather facts and build a case that can be presented in court, ensuring that justice is served while adhering to legal standards and protecting the rights of individuals involved.

3. Public Order Maintenance

Maintaining public order is a fundamental responsibility of law enforcement. This includes managing public events, controlling crowds, and responding to disturbances or riots. Officers are trained to handle these situations in a way that minimises the potential for violence and ensures the safety of all involved. Their presence is essential in preventing disorderly conduct, vandalism, and other forms of disruptive behaviour that can threaten the peace and security of public spaces. Effective public order maintenance also involves coordinating with event organisers and other stakeholders to plan and implement safety measures in advance.

4. Emergency Response

In times of crisis, law enforcement officers are often the first on the scene. Their role in emergency response includes managing accidents, natural disasters, and active crime situations such as shootings or hostage situations. Quick and effective action by law enforcement can save lives, secure dangerous areas, and provide critical assistance to those in need. Officers are trained to assess the situation rapidly, make informed decisions, and work alongside other emergency services like fire and medical teams to coordinate a comprehensive response. Their ability to act under pressure is crucial in mitigating the impact of emergencies.

5. Traffic Control

Traffic control is another essential function of law enforcement. Officers enforce traffic laws, manage the flow of vehicles, and ensure the safety of drivers and pedestrians. They play a key role in reducing road accidents by monitoring speed limits, preventing impaired driving, and addressing reckless behaviour. In the event of a vehicular accident, law enforcement is responsible for securing the scene, investigating the cause, and facilitating the smooth movement of traffic around the incident. By maintaining order on the roads, law enforcement helps prevent congestion and accidents, contributing to public safety.

6. Law Enforcement and Public Trust

The effectiveness of law enforcement is closely tied to the level of trust they have with the public. Building and maintaining this trust requires transparency, accountability, and consistent positive interactions with community members. When law enforcement agencies operate with integrity and fairness, they are more likely to receive cooperation from the public, which is essential for effective policing. Programs that promote community engagement, operations transparency, and misconduct accountability are crucial for sustaining public confidence. A strong relationship between law enforcement and the community helps in crime prevention, as people are likelier to report crimes and cooperate in investigations.

1.7 Glossary

1. Access Control: Mechanisms and policies designed to regulate who can access and use information or resources within a system. This includes authentication (verifying user identity) and authorisation (determining access levels).

2. Antivirus Software: A software designed to detect, prevent, and remove malicious software (malware) from computers and other devices.

3. Attack Vector: The method or pathway cybercriminals use to gain unauthorised access to a system or network. Typical vectors include phishing emails, malware, and unpatched vulnerabilities.

4. Authentication: Verifying a user's or system's identity before granting access to resources. Methods include passwords, biometric scans, and multi-factor authentication (MFA).

5. Authorization: Determining what resources or actions a user or system can access or perform based on their authenticated identity and access rights.

6. Breach: An incident where unauthorised access to Data, systems, or networks occurs, often resulting in Data theft, exposure, or damage.

7. Cyberattack: A deliberate and malicious attempt to disrupt, damage, or gain unauthorised access to a computer system, network, or digital information.

8. Cybersecurity: Protecting computer systems, networks, and Data from cyberattacks, unauthorised access, and damage. It involves implementing policies, technologies, and procedures to safeguard digital assets.

9. Data Encryption: Converting Data into a coded format to prevent unauthorised access. Only authorised users with the correct decryption key can access the original Data.

10. Firewall: A network security device or software that monitors and controls incoming and outgoing network traffic based on predetermined security rules, preventing unauthorised access.

11. Incident Response: The approach and procedures followed to detect, respond to, and recover from a cybersecurity incident or breach. It includes steps like containment, eradication, and recovery.

12. Malware: Malicious software designed to harm, exploit, or otherwise compromise the functionality or security of a computer system or network. Types include viruses, worms, trojans, and ransomware.

13. Multi-Factor Authentication (MFA): A security process that requires users to provide two or more forms of verification to gain access to a system, enhancing the security of user accounts.

14. Phishing: A type of cyberattack where attackers impersonate legitimate entities to deceive individuals into disclosing sensitive information, such as login credentials or financial details.

1.8 Summary

1. Cyberspace and the Internet of Things (IoT): Cyberspace refers to the virtual environment of computer networks and the Internet. The IoT involves interconnected devices that communicate and exchange Data over the internet, increasing efficiency and convenience and raising security and privacy concerns.
2. Cyber Crimes: Cyber crimes are illegal activities conducted through digital means. These include hacking, phishing, identity theft, and various types of fraud. Such crimes exploit the anonymity and reach of the internet to harm individuals, organisations, and governments.
3. Cyber Criminals: Cyber criminals are individuals or groups who commit illegal activities using digital tools. They may include hackers, organised crime groups, and insiders with malicious intent. Their motivations range from financial gain to political activism.
4. Cyber Security Threats: Cyber security threats are potential dangers that compromise the safety of digital systems and Data. Common threats include malware, ransomware, denial-of-service attacks, and vulnerabilities in software. These threats can lead to Data breaches, financial loss, and damage to reputation.
5. Cyber Laws: Cyber laws are regulations and legal frameworks designed to address and manage issues related to cyberspace and digital activities. They cover Data protection, intellectual property, cybercrime penalties, and online conduct. These laws aim to safeguard users and ensure fair practices online.
6. Law Enforcement Roles and Responses: Law enforcement agencies are crucial in combating cybercrime. Their responsibilities include investigating cyber offences, tracking perpetrators, and enforcing cyber laws. They collaborate with other agencies and international bodies to address complex and cross-border cyber threats.

1.9 Previous Year Solved Questions

Question. How does the proliferation of the Internet of Things (IoT) impact the landscape of cyber security threats, and what role do cyber laws and law enforcement play in addressing these challenges? (Mumbai University MCA 2023)

Answer. The proliferation of the Internet of Things (IoT) profoundly impacts the cyber security landscape. With more devices connected to the internet, the attack surface for cybercriminals expands significantly. This creates multiple vulnerabilities that can be exploited through various methods, such as malware, ransomware, or unauthorised access. IoT devices often lack robust security features, making them attractive targets for cyber attacks.

As these threats evolve, cyber laws are critical in providing a regulatory framework to manage and mitigate the risks associated with IoT and cyberspace. These laws set guidelines for Data protection, outline legal responsibilities for securing digital assets, and prescribe penalties for violations. They help create standards for manufacturers and users of IoT devices to follow, which in turn aids in reducing the incidence of cyber crimes.

Law enforcement plays a crucial role in addressing cyber security challenges by investigating incidents, apprehending criminals, and ensuring compliance with cyber laws. They must adapt their techniques and tools to keep pace with cyber criminals' sophisticated methods. This often involves collaboration with other national and international agencies to tackle cross-border cyber crimes. Furthermore, law enforcement agencies are engaged in public education and awareness efforts to help individuals and organisations understand and implement best practices for cyber security.

In summary, the rise of IoT introduces new vulnerabilities and challenges in cyber security, which are addressed through cyber laws and active law enforcement efforts. Both are essential in safeguarding digital environments and ensuring that emerging threats are managed effectively.

Exercises

Exercise 1 – Multiple Choice Questions

1. Which of the following best describes cyberspace?
a) A physical network of computers
b) A virtual environment for information exchange
c) A specific type of software application
d) A single computer system

2. What does the Internet of Things (IoT) refer to?
a) A network of social media platforms
b) A system of interconnected physical devices
c) A collection of online games
d) A set of digital currency systems

Exercise 2 – True/False

1. Cyber crimes only involve financial theft.
2. Law enforcement agencies use digital forensics to investigate cyber crimes.

.

Exercise 3 – Fill in the blanks

1. Cyberspace is a ________ environment where information flows freely.
2. The Internet of Things involves devices connected through the ________.

Exercise 4- Fill in the blanks with two options

1. A cybercriminal might be motivated by ________ or ________.

A. Personal revenge
B. Financial gain
C. Social media engagement
D. Health improvement

2. Advanced Persistent Threats (APTs) are often carried out by ________ or ________.

A. Insiders
B. Hacktivists
C. State-sponsored actors
D. Small businesses

Exercise 5- Rearrange the sentence

1. Cyber criminals/methods and tools / use various / to carry out their activities.
2. Phishing / involves / deceptive practices / tricking individuals.

Exercise 6- Choose the Odd One Out

1. Malware, Phishing, Ransomware, Social Media
2. State-Sponsored Actors, Hacktivists, Identity Theft, Cyber Thieves

Exercise 7- Jumble words

1. SCEYBAPRS
2. NCRTOEINET OF THINGS

Exercise 8- Match case

A. Phishing
B. Ransomware
C. APT
D. Cyber Thieves

1. A type of malware that encrypts Data and demands payment for decryption.
2. Deceptive attempts to acquire sensitive information.
3. Prolonged, targeted attacks, often by sophisticated actors.
4. Individuals motivated primarily by financial gain through theft or fraud..

Exercise 9- Assertion – Reason

1. Assertion: The Internet of Things (IoT) introduces new security challenges. Reason: IoT devices often communicate over cyberspace, which can increase vulnerability.

A. Both Assertion and Reason are correct and Reason is the correct explanation for Assertion.
B. Both Assertion and Reason are correct but Reason is not the correct explanation for Assertion.
C. Assertion is correct but Reason is incorrect.
D. Assertion is incorrect but Reason is correct.

2. Assertion: Cyber laws are designed to address issues related to digital activities. Reason: The rapid pace of technological advancement often makes it difficult to develop corresponding legal frameworks.

A. Both Assertion and Reason are correct and Reason is the correct explanation for Assertion.
B. Both Assertion and Reason are correct but Reason is not the correct explanation for Assertion.

C. Assertion is correct but Reason is incorrect.
D. Assertion is incorrect but Reason is correct.

Exercise 10- Read the questions given below and find the appropriate word in the grid provided.
Questions:

1. Refers to illegal activities conducted through digital means: __________.
2. Potential dangers that compromise the safety of digital systems and Data: __________.

Grid:

C	Y	B	E	R	C	R	I	M	E	N	M	G	E
D	E	F	B	H	R	Q	P	T	Y	K	A	B	V
D	K	E	N	O	I	V	N	G	S	A	L	F	E
S	E	C	U	R	I	T	Y	T	H	R	E	A	T
A	H	V	C	B	E	Q	F	N	L	M	W	J	B
R	M	N	H	S	A	F	G	X	W	O	A	H	A
E	Q	W	E	T	R	C	Y	V	T	P	R	K	L
S	H	I	V	Y	J	K	K	R	S	Q	E	O	M

Exercise 11- One- word

1. What is the term for malicious software that encrypts Data and demands payment?
2. What type of cyber criminal seeks financial gain through theft or fraud?

Exercise 12- Small Answers

1. What does IoT stand for?
2. What is the primary goal of phishing attacks?

Exercise 13- Long Answers

1. Describe the impact of cyber crimes on businesses and individuals.
2. Explain the role of law enforcement in combating cyber crimes and the challenges they face

Exercise 14- Previous Year Unsolved Questions

1. Describe the concept of cyberspace and explain how the Internet of Things (IoT) has expanded the scope of cyberspace. Provide examples. (Mumbai University, December 2023, MCA)
2. Define cybercrime and categorize the different types of cybercrimes. Provide examples of each category. (Mumbai University, December 2023, MCA)
3. Describe the importance of international cooperation in law enforcement responses to cybercrime. Provide examples of successful international collaborations. (Mumbai University, December 2023, MCA)
4. Explain the following in brief:
a) The concept and need for cyber security
b) Types of conventional ciphers
c) Filtering devices and rating systems
d) Difference between cyber crimes and traditional crimes (IGNOU, December 2021, MCA)
5. Discuss the core elements of Data security. (IGNOU, December 2021, MCA)
6. Critically examine the copyright issues in digital medium. (IGNOU, December 2021, MCA)
7. Discuss the law in the United States for regulation of cyberspace. (IGNOU, December 2021, MCA)

Answers

Exercise 1- **1.** B. A virtual environment for information exchange, 2. B. A system of interconnected physical devices

Exercise 2- **1**. False, **2.** True
Exercise 3- **1.** Virtual, **2**. Internet
Exercise 4- **1**. Personal revenge, Financial gain **2**. C. State-sponsored actors, D. Hacktivists
Exercise 5- 1. Cyber criminals use various methods and tools to carry out their activities, **2**. Phishing involves deceptive practices tricking individuals.
Exercise 6- **1.** Social Media, **2.** Identity theft
Exercise 7- **1.** CYBERSPACE **2.** INTERNET OF THINGS
Exercise 8- 1. A – 2 **2.** B – 1 **3.** C – 3 **4.** D - 4
Exercise 9- **1.** A. Both Assertion and Reason are correct and Reason is the correct explanation for Assertion. **2.** A. Both Assertion and Reason are correct and Reason is the correct explanation for Assertion.
Exercise 10- 1. Cyber Crimes, 2. Security Threat

C	Y	B	E	R	C	R	I	M	E	N	M	G	E
D	E	F	B	H	R	Q	P	T	Y	K	A	B	V
D	K	E	N	O	I	V	N	G	S	A	L	F	E
S	E	C	U	R	I	T	Y	T	H	R	E	A	T
A	H	V	C	B	E	Q	F	N	L	M	W	J	B
R	M	N	H	S	A	F	G	X	W	O	A	H	A
E	Q	W	E	T	R	C	Y	V	T	P	R	K	L
S	H	I	V	Y	J	K	K	R	S	Q	E	O	M

Exercise 11- 1. Ransomware **2.** Cyber Thieves

Test Paper

Chapter-1

Introduction to Cyber Security

Time Duration: 30 Minutes **Maximum Marks: 25**

General Instructions:

1. The question paper consists of 12 questions and is divided into four sections, A, B, C and D.
2. All questions are compulsory.
3. Section A comprises MCQs, Fill in the blanks and True or False carrying one marks each.
4. Section B comprises VSAQs(very short answers questions) carrying two marks each.
5. Section C comprises SAQs(short questions) carrying four marks each.
6. Section D comprises long questions carrying five marks each.

SECTION-A

I. Multiple choice questions: **(1*2=2)**

1. Which of the following best defines cyberspace?
a) A place in the digital world where all activities happen
b) A physical space with computer servers
c) A term used for secure communication only
d) None of the above

2. Who are cyber criminals?
a) Individuals engaged in computer-based crimes
b) Individuals developing software
c) Legal experts on cyber laws
d) None of the above

Fill in the blanks: **(1*2=2)**

1. The _____ is a network of interconnected devices embedded with sensors and software that collect and exchange Data.
2. _____ refers to legal frameworks that protect against illegal activities in the digital world.

II. True or False: **(1*2=2)**

1. Cyber crimes always involve financial fraud. (True/False)
2. Law enforcement plays a significant role in responding to cyber security threats. (True/False)

SECTION-B

IV. Very Short answers type questions-I **(2*3=6)**

1. Define cyberspace in simple terms.
2. What are the roles of law enforcement agencies in combating cyber crimes?
3. Briefly explain what is meant by the Internet of Things (IoT).

SECTION-C

V. Short answers type questions-II **(4*2=8)**

1. Explain the major types of cyber security threats with examples.
2. Discuss the importance of cyber laws in today's digital age.

SECTION-D

VI. Long answers type questions **(5*1=5)**

1. Describe the role of law enforcement in preventing and investigating cyber crimes. Provide examples to support your answer.

ONLINE RESOURCES

Practice Paper
Link: https://forms.gle/d6G5QMbufAoG18m4A

QR Code:

YouTube Video Playlist Link
Link: https://www.youtube.com/playlist?list=PLzlh_31VWEFqw6Ah-eeBO1Lwh5Qmq20K_

QR Code:

Chapter 2 - Network Security

In this chapter, you will learn about:
Network Attacks Overview
MITM (Man-In-The-Middle) Attacks
Arp Spoofing
IP & MAC Spoofing
DNS Attacks
SYN Flooding Attacks
DoS and DDoS Attacks
Network Penetration Testing
Firewall and IDS/IPS
Wireless Network Security Protocols

Network security protects the integrity, confidentiality, and availability of Data and resources within a network. As organisations increasingly rely on digital communication and Data storage, safeguarding these assets has become critical to prevent unauthorised access, Data breaches, and cyberattacks.
Network security involves implementing various technologies, policies, and procedures to defend against various threats. These threats can take many forms, including malware, phishing attacks, unauthorised access, and vulnerability exploitation. Network security aims to create a secure environment where information can be transmitted, stored, and accessed safely without falling into the hands of malicious actors.
A robust network security strategy includes several layers of defence. These layers may include firewalls, intrusion detection systems, encryption protocols, and secure access controls. By deploying these mechanisms, organisations can monitor and manage their networks, detect and respond to threats in real-time, and ensure that sensitive Data remains protected.

2.1 Network Attacks Overview

1. Denial of Service (DoS) and Distributed Denial of Service (DDoS)
These attacks aim to disrupt network service availability by overwhelming it with illegitimate requests. In a DoS attack, a single machine sends excessive traffic to the target, exhausting its resources. A DDoS attack is more sophisticated, utilising a network of compromised devices (often called a botnet) to launch a coordinated attack from multiple sources, making it harder to mitigate. The result is a significant slowdown or complete outage of the target service.
2. Phishing
Phishing attacks are a form of social engineering where attackers deceive individuals into providing sensitive information, such as login credentials, financial Data, or personal details. This is usually done by sending fake emails or messages that appear to be from legitimate sources, like banks or online services. Victims are often directed to a counterfeit website that looks identical to the legitimate one, where they unknowingly enter their information, which the attacker then captures.
3. Man-in-the-Middle (MitM) Attacks
In a MitM attack, an attacker secretly intercepts and possibly alters the communication between two parties without their knowledge. The attacker positions themselves between the victim and the legitimate service, gaining access to sensitive Data like passwords or credit card numbers. This can be achieved through various methods, such as exploiting unsecured Wi-Fi networks or hijacking a session.
4. SQL Injection
SQL injection attacks occur when an attacker manipulates a vulnerable web application by injecting malicious SQL code into an input field. This code is then executed by the application's Database, allowing the attacker to view, modify, or delete Data. Such attacks exploit poorly sanitised user inputs and can lead to severe Data breaches, as attackers can gain unauthorized access to the backend Database.
5. Ransomware
Ransomware is malware that encrypts the victim's Data, rendering it inaccessible until a ransom is paid, usually in cryptocurrency. The attacker often threatens to delete or publicly release the Data if the ransom is unpaid. Ransomware attacks can cripple organisations, leading to significant financial losses and operational disruption.

6. Cross-Site Scripting (XSS)

XSS attacks involve injecting malicious scripts into websites executed in the victim's browser. This occurs when a web application does not properly sanitise user input. Attackers can use XSS to steal session cookies, redirect users to malicious sites, or deface web pages. There are three main types of XSS: stored, reflected, and DOM-based, each with different attack mechanisms.

2.2 MITM (Man-In-The-Middle) Attacks

Man-in-the-middle (MitM) attacks are a type of cyberattack in which an attacker secretly intercepts and potentially alters the communication between two parties who believe they are directly communicating. The attacker positions themselves in the middle of the communication channel, gaining access to sensitive information such as login credentials, financial Data, or personal messages.

How Man in the Middle attack works

MitM attacks typically involve several steps:

- **Intercepting the Communication:** The attacker must first intercept the communication between the two parties. This can be done by exploiting network vulnerabilities, such as unsecured Wi-Fi connections, or by employing techniques like DNS spoofing, where the attacker reroutes the communication through their own system.
- **Eavesdropping:** Once the communication is intercepted, the attacker can listen to the conversation and capture any sensitive data transmitted. This can include passwords, credit card numbers, or personal information.
- **Data Manipulation:** Beyond eavesdropping, the attacker can also modify the Data being exchanged between the parties. For example, in an online banking transaction, the attacker could alter the recipient's account number, redirecting the funds to their account.

Types of MitM

There are several common types of MitM attacks, including:

- **Wi-Fi Eavesdropping:** Attackers set up fake Wi-Fi access points or exploit unsecured public Wi-Fi networks to intercept communications.
- **HTTPS Spoofing:** The attacker tricks the victim's browser into believing it is communicating with a secure website when, in fact, the communication is being routed through the attacker's system.
- **Session Hijacking**: The attacker takes over a user's session with a web application by stealing the session token, allowing them to impersonate the user.
- **SSL Stripping:** In this attack, the attacker downgrades the connection from HTTPS to HTTP, making intercepting and manipulating the transmitted data easier.

2.3 Arp Spoofing

ARP Spoofing, or ARP Cache Poisoning, is a cyberattack where an attacker sends falsified Address Resolution Protocol (ARP) messages to a local network. This attack aims to associate the attacker's MAC (Media Access Control) address with the IP address of another device on the network, such as the default gateway. Once prosperous, the attacker can intercept, modify, or even stop Data intended for that IP address.

How ARP Spoofing Works

ARP spoofing exploits how ARP functions in local area networks (LANs). ARP is responsible for mapping IP addresses to MAC addresses, which are necessary for communication devices on the same network. Here's how ARP spoofing typically occurs:

Crafting Fake ARP Messages: The attacker generates and sends forged ARP messages to the network. These messages claim that the attacker's MAC address corresponds to the IP address of a legitimate device, such as the network gateway.

Poisoning the ARP Cache: When devices on the network receive these spoofed ARP messages, they update their ARP cache (a table that stores IP-to-MAC address mappings) with the false information. As a result, any traffic intended for the legitimate IP address is sent to the attacker's device.

Intercepting Traffic: The attacker now sits in the middle of the communication between devices on the network. This allows them to intercept and potentially modify Data packets, perform a Man-In-The-Middle (MitM) attack, or cause a denial of service by dropping the packets entirely.

Impact of ARP Spoofing

The consequences of a successful ARP spoofing attack can be severe, including:

- **Data Interception:** The attacker can capture sensitive information such as login credentials, emails, or Financial Data.
- **Network Disruption:** By altering the traffic flow, the attacker can disrupt normal network operations, causing delays or preventing communication altogether.

• **Session Hijacking:** The attacker can hijack a user's session by capturing session tokens, allowing them to impersonate the user on the network.
• **Facilitation of Other Attacks:** ARP spoofing can be a precursor to more advanced attacks like MitM or denial of service (DoS) attacks.

Prevention and Mitigation

Preventing ARP spoofing requires a combination of technical controls and best practices, including:
• **Static ARP Entries:** Configuring static ARP entries on critical devices ensures malicious actors cannot easily alter their IP-to-MAC address mappings.
• ARP Spoofing Detection Tools: Use of network monitoring tools that can detect and alert suspicious ARP traffic, such as duplicate IP-to-MAC mappings.
• **Encryption:** Implementing robust encryption protocols like HTTPS and SSL/TLS on sensitive communications helps protect Data even if it is intercepted.
• **Network Segmentation:** Segmenting the network into smaller, more secure zones can limit the impact of an ARP spoofing attack to a specific segment.
• **Use of VPNs:** Virtual Private Networks (VPNs) encrypt traffic over potentially vulnerable networks, making it harder for attackers to intercept or manipulate Data.

2.4 IP & MAC Spoofing

IP Spoofing and **MAC Spoofing** are techniques used by attackers to disguise their identity on a network by altering their device's IP or MAC address. These methods are commonly employed in various cyberattacks, such as denial of service (DoS) attacks, man-in-the-middle (MitM) attacks, and to bypass network security measures.

IP Spoofing

IP Spoofing involves creating IP packets with a forged source IP address, making it appear that the packet originated from a different, legitimate source.

How IP Spoofing Works

• **Forging IP Packets:** The attacker crafts IP packets with a fake source IP address, usually one that belongs to a trusted host within the target network.
• **Sending Malicious Traffic**: The spoofed packets are then sent to the target. Because the source IP is forged, the target may treat the packets as legitimate, allowing the attacker to bypass IP-based authentication or filtering mechanisms.
• **Exploiting Trust Relationships:** Many networks have trust relationships based on IP addresses. By spoofing a trusted IP, an attacker can gain unauthorised access to network resources or inject malicious traffic into the network.

Impact of IP Spoofing

• **Bypassing Access Controls:** Attackers can gain unauthorised access to restricted systems by appearing to be a trusted host.
• **Denial of Service (DoS) Attacks: IP** spoofing is commonly used in DoS attacks to overwhelm a target with traffic and make it difficult to trace the attack's origin.
• **Session Hijacking:** Attackers can hijack ongoing communication sessions by spoofing the IP address of one of the parties involved.

Prevention and Mitigation

• **Packet Filtering:** Implementing ingress and egress filtering on routers to drop packets with forged or unexpected IP addresses.
• **IPsec:** Encrypting and authenticating IP packets using IPsec helps ensure that the source IP address is genuine.
• **Network Monitoring:** Monitoring network traffic for anomalies, such as multiple packets with the same IP address from different locations.

MAC Spoofing

MAC Spoofing involves changing the Media Access Control (MAC) address of a network interface on a device. The MAC address is a unique identifier assigned to network interfaces for communications on the physical network segment.

How MAC Spoofing Works

• **Altering MAC Address:** The attacker changes their device's MAC address to match another device on the same network. This can be done using software tools that modify the network interface settings.
• **Assuming the Identity of Another Device:** Once the MAC address is spoofed, the attacker's device can impersonate the legitimate device, receiving network traffic intended for the legitimate device.

• **Exploiting Network Resources:** With the spoofed MAC address, the attacker can gain access to network resources, bypass MAC-based access controls, or disrupt network communication by causing MAC address conflicts.

Impact of MAC Spoofing

• **Network Disruption:** MAC spoofing can cause conflicts on the network, leading to intermittent connectivity issues or loss of network access for legitimate devices.

• **Evasion of Network Security:** Attackers can bypass network security mechanisms that rely on MAC address filtering, such as wireless network access controls.

• **Identity Theft:** The attacker can assume the identity of another device on the network, making it difficult to trace their malicious activities.

Prevention and Mitigation

• **Port Security:** Enabling port security on network switches can limit the number of MAC addresses per port, preventing unauthorized devices from connecting.

• **MAC Address Filtering:** Implementing MAC address filtering can restrict access to the network based on the allowed MAC addresses, though spoofing can bypass this.

• **Network Monitoring:** Continuously monitoring for changes in MAC addresses and detecting duplicate MAC addresses on the network can help identify spoofing attempts.

• **Authentication Mechanisms:** Using more robust authentication mechanisms, such as 802.1X, can help ensure that only authorised devices can connect to the network.

2.5 DNS Attacks.

DNS (Domain Name System) attacks are malicious activities that target the DNS infrastructure. This infrastructure translates human-readable domain names (like www.example.com) into IP addresses (like 192.0.2.1). DNS is essential for the functioning of the Internet, and attacks on this system can have serious implications for both individuals and organisations.

Types of DNS Attacks

1. DNS Spoofing (Cache Poisoning)

Description: DNS spoofing, or cache poisoning, involves injecting incorrect DNS records into a DNS resolver's cache. This cache stores mappings of domain names to IP addresses to speed up subsequent queries. An attacker can manipulate the DNS resolver by poisoning this cache to return false information. When a user tries to visit a domain, the resolver provides the attacker's fraudulent IP address instead of the legitimate one.

Detailed Explanation: The attack begins when the attacker sends many DNS responses to a resolver before the legitimate response arrives. These responses contain fake IP addresses for legitimate domain names. If the resolver accepts these false responses and caches them, subsequent requests for those domain names will be directed to the attacker's IP address. This can lead to users being redirected to malicious websites designed to steal credentials, distribute malware, or perform other harmful activities. Cache poisoning can also redirect traffic intended for a legitimate site to a server controlled by the attacker, where the attacker can then execute additional attacks.

2. DNS Hijacking

Description: DNS hijacking involves redirecting DNS queries from legitimate DNS servers to rogue servers controlled by the attacker. This redirection can occur through various methods, including compromising DNS server configurations, manipulating DNS records, or exploiting vulnerabilities in DNS software.

Detailed Explanation: Attackers can perform DNS hijacking by gaining unauthorized access to a DNS server or by manipulating the domain registrar's settings to point to a malicious DNS server. Once the redirection is in place, any DNS queries made by users are sent to the attacker's server rather than the legitimate one. The rogue DNS server can then provide malicious IP addresses in response to DNS queries. For example, users trying to access their online banking site might be redirected to a phishing site that mimics the legitimate site to capture login credentials. DNS hijacking can also intercept and redirect traffic for other malicious purposes, such as injecting ads, spying on user activity, or conducting further attacks.

3. DNS Amplification

Description: DNS amplification is a type of Distributed Denial of Service (DDoS) attack that exploits DNS servers to amplify the volume of traffic sent to a target. The attacker sends a DNS query to an open DNS resolver with a spoofed IP address, causing the server to respond with a much more significant amount of Data to the victim's IP address.

Detailed Explanation: The attacker sends a small DNS request to an open resolver, with the source IP address spoofed to be that of the victim. The DNS server then sends a much larger response to the victim's IP address, amplifying the attack's impact. This amplification can send a flood of DNS responses to the target, overwhelming their network and causing service disruptions. The attack leverages that DNS responses can be significantly more significant than the initial request, leading to a disproportionate traffic amplification.

4. DNS Tunnelling

Description: DNS tunnelling involves encoding Data within DNS queries and responses to bypass network security measures and establish covert communication channels between a compromised system and an attacker's server.

Detailed Explanation: In a DNS tunnelling attack, the attacker uses DNS queries to exfiltrate Data from a compromised system. The Data is encoded into DNS query packets and sent to a DNS server controlled by the attacker. The DNS server decodes the Data and sends it to the attacker. Similarly, Data from the attacker can be sent back to the compromised system via DNS responses. This technique can bypass traditional network security controls because DNS traffic is often allowed through firewalls and monitoring systems. DNS tunnelling can be used for Data exfiltration, command and control communications, or to establish persistent access to a compromised network.

2.6 SYN Flooding Attacks

SYN Flooding is a Denial of Service (DoS) attack that targets the TCP three-way handshake process to overwhelm a network service or server. This attack exploits how TCP connections are established to exhaust system resources, causing legitimate connection requests to be dropped or delayed.

How SYN Flooding Works

1. TCP Handshake Overview:

Three-Way Handshake: To establish a TCP connection, a three-way handshake occurs:

SYN: The client sends a SYN (synchronise) packet to the server to initiate a connection.

SYN-ACK: The server responds with a SYN-ACK (synchronize-acknowledge) packet, acknowledging the request.

ACK: The client sends an ACK (acknowledge) packet to finalise the connection.

2. Attack Process:

Sending SYN Packets: In a SYN Flooding attack, the attacker sends SYN packets to the target server. These packets have forged source IP addresses, making it difficult to trace the attack.

Server Response: The server responds to each SYN packet with a SYN-ACK packet and allocates resources to handle the incoming connection requests.

Half-Open Connections: Because the source IP addresses are forged or non-existent, the client never completes the handshake by sending the final ACK packet. This leaves the server with numerous half-open connections, where resources are tied up waiting for the final acknowledgement.

3. Resource Exhaustion:

Impact on Resources: As the server continues to allocate resources for the half-open connections, it can exhaust its memory and processing power. This leads to a depletion of available resources and affects the server's ability to handle legitimate connection requests.

Service Disruption: Eventually, the server becomes overwhelmed and may become unresponsive or slow down significantly, disrupting service for legitimate users.

4. Impact of SYN Flooding Attacks

Service Disruption: The primary impact of SYN flooding attacks is the disruption of services, as legitimate users cannot establish new connections to the server.

Resource Depletion: The attack consumes server resources, leading to performance degradation or server crashes.

Denial of Service: Users experience service outages or degraded performance due to the server being unable to handle legitimate connection requests.

2.7 DoS and DDoS Attacks

1. Denial of Service (DoS) Attack

A Denial of Service (DoS) attack is a type of cyberattack aimed at disrupting the normal functioning of a targeted server, service, or network by overwhelming it with a flood of traffic or exploiting specific vulnerabilities. The primary goal of a DoS attack is to exhaust the target's resources—such as bandwidth, CPU, or memory—thereby rendering it unable to respond to legitimate user requests or causing it to crash completely. DoS attacks can be executed in several ways, including sending massive traffic to the target, exploiting protocol vulnerabilities, or causing a service to enter a state where it cannot process legitimate requests.

Key Features:

a. Single Source: Typically originates from a single compromised machine or device.

b. Flood Attack: Involves sending a high volume of Data packets to the target, overwhelming its ability to process and respond.

c. Ping of Death: Uses maliciously crafted ping packets to crash the target system.

d. SYN Flood: Exploits the TCP handshake process by sending numerous SYN requests, overwhelming the target's ability to complete and establish connections.

2. Distributed Denial of Service (DDoS) Attack

A Distributed Denial of Service (DDoS) attack is an advanced form of DoS attack that involves multiple systems—often part of a botnet—coordinated to flood a target with an overwhelming amount of traffic from various sources. This distributed nature of the attack makes it significantly more challenging to mitigate than a traditional DoS attack, as the traffic originates from numerous IP addresses, making it difficult to distinguish between legitimate and malicious requests. DDoS attacks can exploit various vulnerabilities and target different layers of the network stack, from the network infrastructure to specific applications.

Key Features:

a. Multiple Sources: Originates from a network of compromised devices, known as a botnet, which can include computers, I devices, or other networked systems.

b. Volumetric Attack: This type of attack overwhelms the network's bandwidth with massive traffic, such as UDP floods or DNS amplification attacks.

c. Protocol Attack: Exploits weaknesses in network protocols to consume server resources or network infrastructure, such as SYN floods or fragmenting packets.

d. Application Layer Attack: Targets specific applications or services, aiming to exhaust resources at the application level, such as HTTP floods or Slowloris attacks.

Impact:

a. Service Disruption: This can render the target service, website, or network unavailable to legitimate users, leading to operational downtime.

b. Resource Exhaustion: Depletes resources like bandwidth, processing power, and memory, which can degrade performance or cause crashes.

c. Economic and Reputational Damage: Causes financial loss due to downtime and can damage the reputation of the affected organisation.

2.8 Network Penetration Testing

Definition: Network penetration testing, commonly known as "pen testing," is a systematic and controlled process used to identify and evaluate security vulnerabilities in a network. This testing mimics the actions of malicious hackers to uncover weaknesses that attackers could exploit. The goal is to assess the security posture of a network, identify potential vulnerabilities, and recommend measures to mitigate these risks

Objectives:

Identify Vulnerabilities: Detect security weaknesses within the network infrastructure that could be exploited.

Assess Impact: Evaluate the potential impact of exploiting these vulnerabilities on the organisation.

Test Defenses: Examine the effectiveness of existing security controls and defences.

Improve Security Posture: Provide recommendations to enhance network security and reduce the risk of successful attacks.

Phases of Network Penetration Testing:

Planning and Scoping:

Objective Setting: Define the goals and scope of the test, including which systems and networks will be tested.

Permissions and Legalities: Obtain necessary authorisations and meet legal and compliance requirements.

Reconnaissance (Information Gathering):

Passive Reconnaissance: Collect information about the target network without directly interacting with it (e.g., researching publicly available information, domain records).

Active Reconnaissance: Engage with the network to gather information (e.g., network scanning, port scanning) to identify live hosts, open ports, and services.

Scanning and Enumeration:

Network Scanning: Use tools to map the network and identify active devices and services.

Port Scanning: Identify open ports and services on network devices.

Vulnerability Scanning: Automated tools detect known vulnerabilities in services and systems.

Exploitation:

Vulnerability Exploitation: Attempt to exploit identified vulnerabilities to gain unauthorised access or control over network resources.

Privilege Escalation: Attempt to gain higher access or control levels within the network.

Types of Penetration Testing:

Black Box Testing: The tester has no prior knowledge of the network or systems being tested and simulates an external attacker.
White Box Testing: The tester has full knowledge of the network's architecture and source code and simulates an internal or well-informed external attacker.
Gray Box Testing: The tester has partial knowledge of the network, representing a scenario where an attacker has some insider information but is unaware of the system details.

2.9 Firewall and IDS/IPS

A firewall is a network security device or software that monitors and controls incoming and outgoing network traffic based on predetermined security rules. Its primary purpose is to establish a barrier between a trusted internal network and untrusted external networks, such as the Internet, to prevent unauthorised access and mitigate potential threats.

Types:

Packet-Filtering Firewalls: These operate at the network layer and filter traffic based on IP addresses, ports, and protocols. They inspect packets and allow or block them based on rules.
- **Pros**: Simple and fast.
- **Cons**: Limited the ability to inspect payloads and cannot enforce application-level policies.

Stateful Inspection Firewalls: These track the state of active connections and make decisions based on the context of traffic, such as whether a packet is part of an established connection.
- **Pros**: More secure than packet-filtering firewalls as they track connection states.
- **Cons**: More complex and resource-intensive.

Proxy Firewalls act as intermediaries between the internal network and external sources. They receive requests from internal clients and forward them to external servers on behalf of the client.
- **Pros**: Can provide additional features like content filtering and anonymity.
- **Cons**: It may introduce latency and can be a single point of failure.

Next-Generation Firewalls (NGFW) incorporate advanced features such as application awareness, intrusion prevention, and threat intelligence. They operate at multiple layers, including network and application layers.
- **Pros**: Provides comprehensive security and deep packet inspection.
- **Cons**: Can be complex to configure and manage.

Intrusion Detection System (IDS)

Definition: An IDS is a security system designed to detect and alert potential intrusions or malicious activities within a network. It monitors network traffic and system activities for signs of suspicious behaviour or known attack patterns.

Types:
- **Network-Based IDS (NIDS)**: Monitors and analyses network traffic for suspicious patterns or anomalies.
  - **Pros**: Can detect attacks across the entire network.
  - **Cons**: May produce false positives and is limited to detecting threats in network traffic.
- **Host-Based IDS (HIDS)**: Monitors and analyses the behaviour and activities of individual hosts or devices.
  - **Pros**: Provides detailed information about specific devices and their activities.
  - **Cons**: Data is limited to individual hosts.

Intrusion Prevention System (IPS)

Definition: An IPS is an advanced security system that detects potential intrusions and takes proactive measures to prevent or block malicious activities in real-time. It extends the functionality of an IDS by actively responding to detected threats.

Types:
- **Network-Based IPS (NIPS)**: Monitors and analyses network traffic to identify and prevent malicious activity.
  - **Pros**: Can automatically block malicious traffic and mitigate attacks.
  - **Cons**: This may affect network performance and introduce latency.
- **Host-Based IPS (HIPS)**: Protects individual hosts by monitoring their behaviour and preventing malicious activities on the device.
  - **Pros**: Provides detailed protection for individual devices.
  - **Cons**: Requires installation on each host and can be resource-intensive.

Features:
- **Real-Time Blocking**: Automatically blocks or mitigates threats upon detection.
- **Policy Enforcement**: Enforces security policies to prevent unauthorised access and malicious activities.
- **Response Mechanisms**: Blocking IP addresses, terminating connections, or alerting administrators.

2.10 Wireless Network Security Protocols

Wireless network security protocols protect wireless communication from unauthorised access, interception, and tampering. These protocols ensure the confidentiality, integrity, and availability of Data transmitted over wireless networks. Here's an overview of the key wireless network security protocols:

1. WEP (Wired Equivalent Privacy)

Definition: WEP was one of the original security protocols designed for wireless networks to provide a level of security comparable to wired networks. It was introduced as part of the IEEE 802.11 standard.

Key Features:

- **Encryption**: Uses the RC4 stream cipher for encryption.
- **Key Length**: Typically 64-bit or 128-bit keys, with 64-bit keys consisting of a 40-bit key and a 24-bit initialisation vector (IV).

Weaknesses:

- **Vulnerabilities**: Susceptible to several security issues, including weak encryption keys and vulnerabilities in the IV management.
- **Cracking**: Can be cracked relatively quickly using modern tools and techniques.

Status: Obsolete and highly insecure. More secure protocols have largely replaced it.

2. WPA (Wi-Fi Protected Access)

Definition: WPA was introduced as an interim solution to address WEP's security weaknesses. It offers improved encryption and authentication mechanisms.

Key Features:

- **Encryption**: TKIP (Temporal Key Integrity Protocol) addresses the vulnerabilities of WEP's encryption.
- **Authentication**: Implements mechanisms that are improved compared to WEP.

Weaknesses:

- **Security**: Although it improved upon WEP, WPA is not considered fully secure against modern attacks.
- **Cracking**: Vulnerable to sophisticated attacks, mainly if weak passwords are used.

Status: Superseded by WPA2, but still found in some older networks.

3. WPA2 (Wi-Fi Protected Access II)

Definition: WPA2 is the successor to WPA and is widely used to secure wireless networks. It provides stronger security through more robust encryption and authentication mechanisms.

Key Features:

- **Encryption**: Uses AES (Advanced Encryption Standard) for stronger encryption than TKIP.
- **Authentication**: Supports both WPA2-Personal (PSK) and WPA2-Enterprise (EAP) modes.

WPA2-Personal (PSK):

- **Pre-Shared Key**: Uses a passphrase for authentication.
- **Suitability**: Suitable for home and small office environments.

WPA2-Enterprise (EAP):

- **Extensible Authentication Protocol**: Provides enterprise-level security using methods like EAP-TLS, EAP-TTLS, and PEAP.
- **Suitability**: Designed for larger organisations requiring stronger authentication.

Weaknesses:

- **Vulnerabilities**: While WPA2 is robust, it has been found to be vulnerable to certain types of attacks, such as KRACK (Key Reinstallation Attacks).

Status: Widely used and generally considered secure, though WPA3 is available as a more advanced alternative.

4. WPA3 (Wi-Fi Protected Access III)

Definition: WPA3 is the latest security protocol introduced to enhance the security of wireless networks beyond WPA2. It offers more robust encryption, improved protection against brute-force attacks, and enhanced privacy features.

Key Features:

- **Encryption**: Uses SAE (Simultaneous Authentication of Equals) for more robust protection during the authentication process.
- **Encryption Upgrade**: This uses a 192-bit encryption suite for WPA3-Enterprise.
- **Protection Against Brute-Force Attacks**: Includes safeguards against offline dictionary attacks.

WPA3-Personal:

- **Enhanced Security**: Uses a more secure password-based authentication mechanism with SAE.

WPA3-Enterprise:

Stronger Encryption: Provides a 192-bit security suite for higher levels of protection in enterprise environments.

Weaknesses:

Adoption: Requires newer hardware and firmware; older devices may not support WPA3.

Status: Emerging standard with increasing adoption; considered the most secure wireless protocol available.

5. 802.1X

Definition: 802.1X is an IEEE standard for network access control, often used with WPA/WPA2/WPA3 to provide enterprise-level security. It uses the Extensible Authentication Protocol (EAP) to provide robust authentication for network access.

Key Features:

Authentication: Use EAP-TLS (Transport Layer Security) and EAP-TTLS (Tunneled Transport Layer Security) for secure authentication.

Access Control: Controls access to network resources based on authentication.

Status: Widely used in enterprise environments for network access control.

2.11 Glossary

• Access Control: Mechanisms and policies used to restrict access to resources and systems based on authentication and authorisation.
• ARP Spoofing: An attack where a malicious actor sends falsified Address Resolution Protocol (ARP) messages to associate their MAC address with the IP address of another device, leading to network traffic interception or redirection.
• DoS (Denial of Service) Attack: A cyberattack aimed at making a network service, website, or system unavailable by overwhelming it with excessive traffic or requests.
• DDoS (Distributed Denial of Service) Attack: A form of DoS attack where multiple compromised systems simultaneously flood a target with traffic, making it difficult to mitigate due to the distributed nature of the attack.
• DNS Attack: An attack targeting the Domain Name System (DNS) to manipulate or intercept DNS queries and responses, potentially redirecting traffic or causing service disruptions.
• Exploitation: The process of taking advantage of a vulnerability in a system to gain unauthorised access or control.
• Firewall: A network security device or software that monitors and controls incoming and outgoing network traffic based on predetermined security rules.
• IDS (Intrusion Detection System): A security system that monitors network traffic and system activities for signs of malicious activity or policy violations, alerting administrators of potential threats.
• IPS (Intrusion Prevention System): An advanced security system that detects potential intrusions and proactively prevents or blocks malicious activities in real-time.
• MAC Spoofing: The act of altering or falsifying a device's MAC (Media Access Control) address to impersonate another device on a network.
• MITM (Man-In-The-Middle) Attack: An attack where an attacker intercepts and potentially alters the communication between two parties without their knowledge.
• NAT (Network Address Translation): A technique used by firewalls to hide internal IP addresses from external networks, allowing multiple devices to share a single public IP address.
• Packet-Filtering Firewall: A type of firewall that examines packets of Data and allows or blocks them based on IP addresses, ports, and protocols.
• Penetration Testing (Pen Testing): A systematic process used to identify and evaluate network security vulnerabilities by simulating potential attackers' actions.
• Port Scanning: Identifying open ports on a networked device to determine which services are available and potentially vulnerable.
• Protocol Attack: A type of DDoS attack that exploits weaknesses in network protocols to consume resources and disrupt network services.
• SYN Flood: A type of DoS attack that exploits the TCP handshake process by sending numerous SYN requests to overwhelm a system's ability to handle connections.
• WEP (Wired Equivalent Privacy): An obsolete wireless security protocol designed to provide a level of security comparable to wired networks but is now considered insecure.
• WPA (Wi-Fi Protected Access): A wireless security protocol that improved upon WEP by using TKIP (Temporal Key Integrity Protocol) for better encryption and authentication.

• WPA2 (Wi-Fi Protected Access II): The successor to WPA, providing stronger security through AES (Advanced Encryption Standard) encryption and improved authentication methods.
• WPA3 (Wi-Fi Protected Access III): The latest wireless security protocol offering enhanced security features, such as more robust encryption and better protection against brute-force attacks.
• Wireless Network Security Protocols: Standards and protocols designed to secure wireless communication by ensuring Data confidentiality, integrity, and authentication.
• Wireless Access Point (WAP): A hardware device that allows wireless devices to connect to a wired network using Wi-Fi.

2.12 Summary

This chapter provides a comprehensive overview of various aspects of network security, focusing on different types of network attacks, security protocols, and protective measures.
1. Network Attacks Overview: Network attacks are deliberate attempts to disrupt, damage, or gain unauthorised access to a network or its resources. Understanding the different types of attacks is crucial for implementing effective security measures.
2. MITM (Man-In-The-Middle) Attacks: MITM attacks involve an attacker intercepting and potentially altering communication between two parties without their knowledge. This type of attack can compromise sensitive information and manipulate Data.
3. ARP Spoofing: ARP Spoofing is a technique where malicious actors send falsified Address Resolution Protocol (ARP) messages to associate their MAC address with the IP address of another device. This can lead to Data interception or network traffic redirection.
4. IP & MAC Spoofing: IP and MAC spoofing involves falsifying IP or MAC addresses to impersonate another device on a network. These techniques bypass security controls, gain unauthorised access, or disrupt network operations.
5. DNS Attacks: DNS attacks target the Domain Name System (DNS) to manipulate or intercept DNS queries and responses, potentially redirecting users to malicious sites or disrupting network services.
6. SYN Flooding Attacks: SYN Flooding is a DoS attack that exploits the TCP handshake process by sending numerous SYN requests to overwhelm a system's ability to handle new connections, leading to service disruption.
7. DoS and DDoS Attacks: Denial of Service (DoS) attacks aim to make a network service or system unavailable by flooding it with excessive traffic. Distributed Denial of Service (DDoS) attacks involve multiple compromised systems to launch a coordinated attack, making it harder to mitigate.
8. Network Penetration Testing: Network penetration testing, or pen testing, involves simulating attacks to identify and evaluate vulnerabilities within a network. This proactive approach helps assess security defences and improve overall security posture.
9. Firewall and IDS/IPS: Firewalls are security devices that monitor and control network traffic based on predefined rules. Intrusion Detection Systems (IDS) monitor suspicious activity, while Intrusion Prevention Systems (IPS) actively prevent or block malicious activities. Both play vital roles in network security.
10. Wireless Network Security Protocols: Wireless network security protocols, such as WEP, WPA, WPA2, and WPA3, are designed to protect wireless communications. Each protocol offers different levels of security, with WPA3 providing the most advanced protection against modern threats.
11. This chapter equips readers with essential knowledge on securing network infrastructures by understanding various attacks, implementing protective measures, and utilising effective security protocols.

2.13 Previous Year Solved Questions

Question. How do Intrusion Detection Systems (IDS) and Intrusion Prevention Systems (IPS) differ in their approach to network security, and what are the key advantages and limitations of each? (Udaipur University, MCA 2022)
Answer. Intrusion Detection Systems (IDS) and Intrusion Prevention Systems (IPS) are critical components in a comprehensive network security strategy, but they serve distinct roles and operate differently.
Differences in Approach
Intrusion Detection Systems (IDS):
• **Function:** IDS monitors network traffic and system activities for signs of malicious activity or policy violations. Its primary role is to detect and alert administrators to potential security incidents.
• **Detection Methods:** IDS typically uses two primary methods for detecting threats.
• **Signature-Based Detection:** Identifies known threats by comparing network activity to a Database of attack signatures.
• **Anomaly-Based Detection:** Detects deviations from standard behaviour patterns, indicating unknown threats or suspicious activities.

• **Response:** IDS does not actively block or prevent attacks. Instead, it generates alerts for further investigation and response by security personnel.

Intrusion Prevention Systems (IPS):
• Function: IPS detects potential intrusions and proactively blocks or prevents malicious activities in real-time. It integrates detection with automated response capabilities.
• Detection and Prevention: IPS uses detection methods similar to IDS (signature-based and anomaly-based) but with additional functionality to actively prevent identified threats. This can include:
o Blocking Traffic: Automatically blocking malicious traffic or terminating malicious connections.
o Policy Enforcement: Enforcing security policies to prevent unauthorised access or actions.
•Response: IPS takes immediate action to mitigate threats, reducing the need for manual intervention.

Advantages and Limitations
IDS Advantages:
• Detailed Monitoring: Provides in-depth visibility into network and system activities, allowing for detailed analysis of potential threats.
• Flexibility: Can be used in various network segments to monitor and alert on suspicious activities without affecting network performance.
• No Impact on Traffic: IDS does not alter or block network traffic, which means it does not impact legitimate network operations.
IDS Limitations:
• Reactive Nature: IDS only alerts on potential threats without taking direct action to prevent them, which may delay response and remediation.
• False Positives: Can generate false positives, requiring manual investigation and validation by security teams.
IPS Advantages:
• Proactive Protection: Provides active protection by blocking or mitigating threats in real-time, reducing the risk of successful attacks.
• Policy Enforcement: Can enforce security policies automatically, ensuring consistent application of security controls.
• Reduced Response Time: Minimizes threat detection and mitigation time, enhancing overall security posture.
IPS Limitations
• Performance Impact: This may introduce latency or performance issues due to the processing required for real-time threat prevention and traffic analysis.
• Complex Configuration: Requires careful configuration to avoid blocking legitimate traffic and generating false positives.
• Single Point of Failure: If not properly managed, an IPS could become a single point of failure if it fails to detect or block a threat effectively.

Exercises

Exercise 1 – Multiple Choice Questions

1. What type of attack involves multiple compromised systems flooding a target with traffic?
a) DoS Attack
b) DDoS Attack
c) MITM Attack
d) ARP Spoofing

2. Which security protocol is considered the most advanced for protecting wireless communications?
a) WPA
b) WEP
c) WPA2
d) WPA3

Exercise 2 – True/False

1. ARP Spoofing is a technique used to associate an attacker's MAC address with the IP address of another device.

2. A firewall is a device that actively prevents or blocks malicious activities in real-time.

Exercise 3 – Fill in the blanks

1. A ________ firewall tracks the state of active connections and makes decisions based on the context of traffic.
2. DNS attacks are targeted at the ________ Name System to manipulate or intercept queries and responses.

Exercise 4- Fill in the blanks with two options

1. ________ and ________ are both types of spoofing attacks used to impersonate devices on a network.
(IP / MAC, Firewall / DNS)
2. ________ is an obsolete wireless security protocol, while ________ is the most recent version offering enhanced protection.
(WEP / WPA3, WPA / WPA2)

Exercise 5- Rearrange the sentence

1. security / attacks / Wireless / protect / protocols / are / to / network
2. spoofing / used / to / addresses / is / falsify / MAC / an attack

Exercise 6 – Choose the Odd One Out

1. a) WPA
b) WEP
c) MITM
d) WPA2
2. a) Penetration Testing
b) ARP Spoofing
c) SYN Flood
d) DoS Attack

Exercise 7- Jumble words

1. PSA: ________ (Used to intercept communication between two parties)
MITM, WPA, SYN
2. DCNITIEO: ________ (Used to identify network vulnerabilities)
Packet-Filtering Firewall, Exploitation, Penetration Testing

Exercise 8- Match case

1. SYN Flood
2. WEP
3. ARP Spoofing
4. MITM Attack

a) A type of attack that exploits the TCP handshake process
b) Obsolete wireless security protocol
c) Sends falsified ARP messages to intercept or redirect network traffic
d) Intercepts and alters communication between two parties

Exercise 9- Assertion – Reason

1. Assertion: WPA3 is considered the most secure wireless protocol.
Reason: It uses stronger encryption and better protection against brute-force attacks.
a) Both Assertion and Reason are correct and Reason is the correct explanation for Assertion.
b) Both Assertion and Reason are correct but Reason is not the correct explanation for Assertion.
c) Assertion is correct but Reason is incorrect.
d) Assertion is incorrect but Reason is correct.

2. Assertion: Penetration Testing is used to find vulnerabilities in a network.

Reason: It is done by simulating attacks similar to those used by real attackers.

a) Both Assertion and Reason are correct and Reason is the correct explanation for Assertion.
b) Both Assertion and Reason are correct but Reason is not the correct explanation for Assertion.
c) Assertion is correct but Reason is incorrect.
d) Assertion is incorrect but Reason is correct.

Exercise 10- Read the questions given below and find the appropriate word in the grid provided.
Questions:

1. The attack where an attacker intercepts and potentially alters communication between two parties without their knowledge is called __________.
2. The technique involving falsified Address Resolution Protocol (ARP) messages to associate a MAC address with another IP address is known as __________.

Grid:

M	H	O	A	I	J	B	J	Q	N	C
I	E	F	R	H	Z	Q	P	L	K	V
M	K	E	P	O	P	V	N	M	P	E
T	A	I	S	N	E	S	S	N	O	R
A	R	P	S	P	O	O	F	I	N	G
T	M	N	O	S	A	F	G	H	K	A
T	Q	W	O	T	R	C	Y	G	W	L
A	W	D	F	N	B	T	Y	U	Z	K
C	V	B	I	W	F	B	N	A	X	J
K	H	I	V	Y	J	K	K	D	C	M

Exercise 11- One- word

1. What is the act of gaining unauthorized access by taking advantage of a vulnerability?
2. Which attack exploits the TCP handshake process?

Exercise 12- Small Answers

1. Explain how ARP Spoofing works.
2. What is the difference between DoS and DDoS attacks?

Exercise 13- Long Answers

1. Describe the key differences between WPA, WPA2, and WPA3 in terms of wireless network security.
2. Discuss how Intrusion Detection Systems (IDS) and Intrusion Prevention Systems (IPS) function in protecting a network.

Exercise 14- Previous Year Unsolved Questions

1. Discuss security issues in Cyberspace. (IGNOU, June 2022, MCA)
2. Write a note on Cyber Forensics. (IGNOU, June 2022, MCA)
3. Give an overview of Cyberspace regulation in India. (IGNOU, June 2022, MCA)
4. Explain the following in brief:
a) Digital Signature
b) Pros and Cons of Digital Security
c) Cyber Security Threats
d) UNCITRAL Model Law (IGNOU, June 2022, MCA)
5. Discuss the conditions under which a person is liable to pay damages for violating the provisions of the Information Technology Act, 2000. (IGNOU, June 2022, MCA)
6. "Authentication is one of the most important of all information security objectives." Critically examine the statement. (IGNOU, June 2022, MCA)
7. a) Explain the classification of cybercrimes with examples.

b) Explain phishing and identity theft in detail. (Mumbai University, December 2023, MCA)

8. Explain different buffer overflow attacks also explain how to mitigate buffer overflow attack. (Mumbai University, December 2023, MCA)

Answers

Exercise 1- 1. b) DDoS Attack, 2. **d)** WPA3
Exercise 2- 1. True, 2. False
Exercise 3- 1. Stateful Inspection, 2. Domain.
Exercise 4- 1. IP, MAC, 2. WEP, WPA3
Exercise 5- Wireless network security protocols are to protect attacks, 2. MAC spoofing is used to falsify addresses.
Exercise 6- 1. c) MITM (The rest are security protocols, 2. **a)** Penetration Testing (The rest are types of network attacks.)
Exercise 7- 1. MITM (Man-in-the-Middle), 2. Penetration Testing
Exercise 8- 1 – a, 2 – b, 3 – c, 4 – d
Exercise 9- 1. Both A and R are true and R is the correct explanation, 2. Both A and R are true and R is the correct explanation.
Exercise 10- 1. MITM ATTACK, 2. ARP SPOOFING

M	H	O	A	I	J	B	J	Q	N	C
I	E	F	R	H	Z	Q	P	L	K	V
M	K	E	P	O	P	V	N	M	P	E
T	A	I	S	N	E	S	S	N	O	R
A	R	P	S	P	O	O	F	I	N	G
T	M	N	O	S	A	F	G	H	K	A
T	Q	W	O	T	R	C	Y	G	W	L
A	W	D	F	N	B	T	Y	U	Z	K
C	V	B	I	W	F	B	N	A	X	J
K	H	I	V	Y	J	K	K	D	C	M

Exercise 11- 1. Exploitation, 2. SYN Flood

Test Paper

Chapter-2

Network Security

Time Duration: 30 Minutes **Maximum Marks: 25**

General Instructions:

1. The paper consists of 12 questions and is divided into four sections: A, B, C and D.
2. All questions are compulsory.
3. Section A comprises MCQs: fill in the blanks and True or False, carrying one mark each.
4. Section B comprises VSAQs (very short answer questions) carrying two marks each.
5. Section C comprises five SAQs (short questions) with four marks each.
6. Section D comprises long questions carrying five marks each.

SECTION-A

I. Multiple choice questions: **(1*2=2)**

1. Which attack involves overwhelming a system with excessive traffic to make it unavailable?

a) SYN Flood
b) DNS Attack
c) ARP Spoofing
d) MITM Attack

2. What does the acronym "IPS" stand for?

a) Intrusion Prevention System
b) Internet Protection System
c) Internal Protection Software
d) Intruder Prevention Software

II. Fill in the blanks: **(1*2=2)**

1. __________ is a technique used to hide internal IP addresses by using a single public IP address.
2. The process of sending falsified ARP messages to intercept or redirect network traffic is known as __________.

III. True or False: **(1*2=2)**

1. WEP is the most recent wireless security protocol.
2. A Firewall only detects potential security threats without taking any action.

SECTION-B

IV. Very Short answers type questions- **(2*3=6)**

1. Define ARP Spoofing.
2. What is the primary purpose of a Firewall in network security?
3. Explain the term "Packet Filtering Firewall".

SECTION-C

V. Short answers type questions- **(4*2=8)**

1. Describe the differences between DoS and DDoS attacks.
2. What are the key features of WPA3 compared to WPA2?

SECTION-D

VI. Long answers type **(5*1=5)**

1. Discuss the role of Intrusion Detection Systems (IDS) and Intrusion Prevention Systems (IPS) in network security. Include their differences and how they contribute to protecting a network.

ONLINE RESOURCES

Practice Paper
Link: https://forms.gle/Rhx7vYq2uWAkSTXu5
QR Code:

YouTube Video Playlist Link
Link:
https://www.youtube.com/playlist?list=PLzlh_31VWEFqeuC6U2ueE1kVARD8WTeKJ

QR Code:

Chapter 3 - Web Application Security

In this chapter you will learn about:

Introduction to Web Applications
Cookies and Session Headers
OWASP Top 10 Flaws
Security Fundamentals: Input Validation
Attack Surface Reduction
Vulnerability Assessment
Defensive Software Architecture
Comprehensive Code Reviews

In today's digital landscape, web applications have become an integral part of our lives, facilitating communication, commerce, entertainment, and much more. From online banking and shopping to social media platforms and cloud services, web applications empower both individuals and businesses to operate more efficiently and effectively. However, with the growing reliance on web technologies, the risks associated with their security have also escalated, making web application security a critical area of focus.

3.1 Cookies and Session Headers

Cookies and session headers play a vital role in the communication between a web browser and a server, especially in maintaining stateful interactions in web applications. Understanding how they work and the security implications involved is essential for protecting web applications from various attacks, such as session hijacking, cross-site scripting (XSS), and cross-site request forgery (CSRF).

3.1.1 What Are Cookies?

A cookie is a small piece of Data that a server sends to a user's browser. The browser stores this Data and sends it back to the server with subsequent requests. Cookies allow servers to recognise users and maintain their session across multiple interactions.

Types of Cookies:

- **Session Cookies**: These temporary cookies are deleted when the browser is closed. They are typically used to store session Data during a user's visit to a site.
- **Persistent Cookies:** These remain on the user's device even after the browser is closed, often used for remembering login credentials or user preferences.
- **Secure Cookies:** Sent only over HTTPS connections, ensuring the Data is encrypted in transit.
- **HTTP Only Cookies:** These are not accessible via JavaScript, which helps mitigate the risk of client-side script attacks, like XSS.

Key Attributes of Cookies:

- Domain: Specifies which domain the cookie is valid for.
- Path: Defines the path within the domain where the cookie is valid.
- Expiration: Dictates when the cookie will expire, which is essential for both session management and security.
- SameSite: Controls whether cookies are sent with cross-site requests, which can help defend against CSRF attacks.

3.1.2 Session Management

Sessions refer to the mechanism that allows a server to remember the state of a user's interaction across multiple requests. Since HTTP is a stateless protocol, maintaining session information between the client and server requires specific mechanisms, such as cookies or session headers.

When a user logs into a web application, the server creates a unique session ID and sends it to the client, often stored in a cookie. Each subsequent request from the client includes this session ID, allowing the server to associate the request with the correct user session.

Session Security:

- Session Hijacking: If an attacker gains access to a user's session ID, they can impersonate the user. Mitigations include regenerating session IDs after login, limiting session duration, and using secure cookie attributes.
- Session Fixation: An attack where a user is tricked into using a session ID that the attacker knows. Mitigation includes regenerating session IDs when a user authenticates.

3.1.3 Security Headers for Sessions

Security headers are instructions the server sends to the browser to enforce security-related policies. Certain headers are crucial in enhancing security regarding cookies and session management.

Common Session-Related Headers:

• Set-Cookie: This instructs the browser to store a cookie. Essential attributes like Secure, HTTP Only, and Same Site are often included here.

• Authorization: Carries credentials (such as tokens) to authenticate a user session without cookies.

• X-Frame-Options: Prevents clickjacking attacks by controlling whether a web page can be embedded in an iframe.

• Content-Security-Policy (CSP): This policy helps mitigate XSS by controlling the sources from which scripts, styles, and other resources can be loaded.

3.2 OWASP Top 10 Flaws

The Open Web Application Security Project (OWASP) Top 10 is a globally recognised standard for web application security. It represents the most critical security risks to web applications, guiding the most common vulnerabilities and how to address them. Below is an overview of the OWASP Top 10 security flaws:

1. Broken Access Control

Access control ensures that users can only perform actions and access resources they are authorised for. Broken access control occurs when restrictions are not properly enforced, allowing attackers to gain unauthorised access.

Common Issues:

- Bypassing user roles and permissions.
- Accessing sensitive information (e.g., other users' Data) without proper authorisation.
- Modifying or deleting Data that the user shouldn't have access to.

Mitigations:

- Enforce strong access control mechanisms.
- Implement least privilege and deny-by-default policies.
- Regularly audit and test access control rules.

2. Cryptographic Failures

Formerly known as "Sensitive Data Exposure," this flaw refers to improper cryptography handling, which can expose sensitive information such as passwords, credit card numbers, or personal Data.

Common Issues:

- Weak encryption or hashing algorithms.
- Failure to encrypt sensitive Data in transit or at rest.
- Insecure storage of encryption keys.

Mitigations:

- Use robust and industry-standard encryption algorithms.
- Enable HTTPS for all sensitive Data transmissions.
- Securely manage and store encryption keys.

3. Injection

Injection flaws, such as SQL, NoSQL, or LDAP injection, occur when untrusted Data is sent to an interpreter as part of a command or query. This allows attackers to execute malicious code or queries.

Common Issues:

- SQL Injection (SQLi) through unsanitized input.
- Command Injection through shell commands.
- NoSQL Injection in non-relational Databases.

Mitigations:

- Use parameterised queries and prepared statements.
- Validate and sanitise all input.
- Use Object-Relational Mapping (ORM) frameworks to avoid direct queries.

4. Insecure Design

This focuses on security issues introduced at the design stage, often due to poor threat modelling, insufficient architectural design, or lack of security controls integrated into the application development process.

Common Issues:

- Lack of design for authentication, logging, and session management.
- Failure to anticipate security threats.
- Absence of secure coding practices from the start.

Mitigations:

- Security in the design process.

- Incorporate and Perform threat modelling and design reviews.
- Use secure design patterns and frameworks.

5. Security Misconfiguration

Security misconfigurations happen when security settings are either improperly configured or left at their default values, leaving systems vulnerable to attacks.

Common Issues:

- Using default or weak credentials.
- Unnecessary services or features enabled (e.g., verbose error messages).
- Improper configuration of web server or application software.

Mitigations:

- Regularly review and update configurations.
- Harden systems by disabling unnecessary services and features.
- Use security configuration guides and tools like CIS Benchmarks.

6. Vulnerable and Outdated Components

Using outdated software components or dependencies can introduce known vulnerabilities into an application, exposing it to attacks.

Common Issues:

- Outdated libraries, frameworks, or APIs.
- Unsupported or unpatched third-party software.
- Lack of version tracking and updates.

Mitigations:

- Regularly update all dependencies and software components.
- Use vulnerability management tools to track known issues.
- Adopt automated security updates wherever possible.

7. Identification and Authentication Failures

This category includes flaws related to authentication mechanisms, such as poor password policies, session management vulnerabilities, or improper user authentication.

Common Issues:

- Weak or default passwords.
- Insufficient multi-factor authentication (MFA) requirements.
- Session hijacking or fixation attacks.

Mitigations:

- Implement robust password policies and multi-factor authentication (MFA).
- Secure session management (e.g., regenerate session IDs after login).
- Use proven authentication frameworks and libraries.

8. Software and Data Integrity Failures

This flaw occurs when software updates, critical Data, or CI/CD pipelines are not adequately protected, leading to unauthorised manipulation or tampering.

Common Issues:

- Use of unsigned or unverified software updates.
- Compromise of CI/CD pipelines or deployment processes.
- Lack of integrity checks for transmitted Data.

Mitigations:

- Use signed software packages and updates.
- Implement code integrity checks.
- Secure the CI/CD pipeline against attacks.

9. Security Logging and Monitoring Failures

Insufficient logging and monitoring can allow attackers to exploit vulnerabilities without detection. Proper logging can also make it difficult to detect and respond to breaches.

Common Issues:

- Lack of logging for critical events (e.g., failed logins, privilege changes).
- Logs not being monitored or reviewed.
- Poorly configured or insecure logging storage.

Mitigations:

- Enable detailed logging for security-related events.

- Implement real-time monitoring and alerting systems.
- Regularly review and audit logs for suspicious activity.

10. Server-Side Request Forgery (SSRF)

SSRF vulnerabilities occur when an application allows an attacker to make unauthorised requests to internal or external systems. This can be exploited to access internal services or bypass firewalls.

Common Issues:

- Allowing external URLs to be passed unchecked to the server.
- Lack of proper input validation for user-supplied URLs.
- Exposing internal services to untrusted external requests.

Mitigations:

- Validate and sanitise all user inputs, especially URLs.
- Use network segmentation to limit access to internal services.
- Implement whitelisting for allowable URLs.

3.3 Security Fundamentals: Input Validation

Introduction to Input Validation

Input validation is one of the most critical security practices in web application development. It ensures that Data received from users or external sources conforms to expected formats and values. Failure to validate input properly can expose applications to attacks such as SQL injection, cross-site scripting (XSS), command injection, and buffer overflow.

Proper input validation helps ensure that user input does not compromise an application's integrity, availability, or confidentiality, safeguarding it from malicious input that could exploit vulnerabilities.

Why Input Validation is Important

Web applications interact with users through various input forms, such as login forms, search boxes, file uploads, and API requests. Without input validation, attackers can manipulate these inputs to send harmful Data to the application or its underlying systems. Proper validation is key to:

- Preventing Injection Attacks: Malicious inputs that manipulate Databases or command execution.
- Ensuring Data Integrity: Protecting the consistency and reliability of Data.
- Blocking Malformed Requests: Rejecting invalid inputs to maintain application functionality and stability.

Types of Input Validation

There arc two primary approaches to input validation:

1. **Client-Side Validation: This** is performed in the user's browser using JavaScript or HTML5. It can improve the user experience by providing instant feedback on invalid inputs but should never be relied upon as a security measure since attackers can bypass it.
2. **Server-Side Validation:** This is performed on the server, where input Data is processed securely. It is crucial because attackers sending requests directly to the server can bypass client-side validation.

Key Input Validation Techniques

1. Whitelisting (Preferred Approach)

- o Whitelisting involves specifying a set of allowed inputs and rejecting anything that doesn't match the predefined rules. This approach is far more secure than blacklisting because it defines what is acceptable, reducing the chance of oversight.
- o Example: Allowing only alphanumeric characters in a username field or only positive integers in a quantity field.

2. Blacklisting (Less Secure)

- o Blacklisting involves defining a list of known dangerous inputs and rejecting them. However, this method is not as reliable because attackers can find ways to bypass the blacklist.
- o Example: Blocking specific characters like < and > to prevent XSS attacks.

3. Data Type Validation

- o Ensure that inputs match the expected Data types (e.g., integers, strings, email addresses, dates). By enforcing strict Data types, applications can prevent specific injection attacks.
- o Example: An age field should accept only integers within a valid range (e.g., 0–120).

4. Length Validation

- o Limiting the length of input fields helps prevent buffer overflows and denial of service (DoS) attacks caused by excessively long inputs.
- o Example: Limiting username fields to a maximum of 30 characters.

Common Attacks Prevented by Input Validation

1. **SQL Injection**
    - o SQL injection occurs when an attacker inserts malicious SQL code into an input field, tricking the Database into executing unintended queries.
    - o Mitigation: Use parameterised queries, prepared statements, and input validation to ensure only expected Data is accepted.
2. **Cross-Site Scripting (XSS)**
    - o XSS allows attackers to inject malicious scripts into web pages viewed by other users.
    - o Mitigation: Validate and sanitise all user input, especially when rendering content in HTML.
3. **Command Injection**
    - o Command injection happens when user input is passed to system-level commands, allowing an attacker to execute arbitrary commands on the server.
    - o Mitigation: Validate input to prevent special characters or dangerous input patterns from being processed.
4. **Cross-Site Request Forgery (CSRF)**
    - o CSRF tricks users into submitting requests they did not intend, often exploiting input fields that are not properly validated.
    - o Mitigation: Use anti-CSRF tokens and input validation to ensure legitimate requests.

3.4 Attack Surface Reduction

Introduction to Attack Surface Reduction

Attack surface reduction means minimising the number of entry points or vulnerabilities an attacker could potentially exploit in a system, network, or application. The larger the attack surface, the more opportunities an attacker has to find and exploit weaknesses. By reducing the attack surface, organisations limit the possible avenues for attack, thus improving security.

The goal of attack surface reduction is to reduce complexity, remove unnecessary functionality, and minimise the number of exposure points to potential threats while maintaining the system or application's required functionality.

Key Concepts in Attack Surface Reduction

1. Attack Surface: The attack surface is the sum of all potential points where an unauthorised user (attacker) could interact with a system. This includes software vulnerabilities, exposed APIs, user inputs, open ports, or any interfaces that could be manipulated.

2. Attack Vector: An attack vector is a path or means by which an attacker gains unauthorised access to a system. Reducing the attack surface limits the number of possible attack vectors.

Strategies for Attack Surface Reduction

1. Minimize Code and Complexity

• Remove Unnecessary Features: Applications often contain features that are not critical for core functionality but expand the attack surface. By removing or disabling these unnecessary features, you reduce potential vulnerabilities.

o Example: Disabling file upload functionality on a web form if not required.

• Simplify Code: Complex systems are more complicated to secure, often introducing hidden vulnerabilities. Simplifying code and reducing the number of external dependencies helps reduce risk.

o Example: Use simple and efficient algorithms instead of complex, inefficient ones that might be harder to secure.

2. Limit User Privileges

• Principle of Least Privilege (PoLP): Ensure that users, processes, and services have only the permissions they need to perform their tasks. Limiting permissions reduces the risk of privilege escalation attacks.

o Example: A user with view-only access should not be able to modify or delete sensitive Data.

• Role-Based Access Control (RBAC): Implementing RBAC ensures that users are assigned roles with specific privileges, which limits unauthorised access to critical systems or Data.

o Example: A customer support representative should have access only to customer service tools, not backend administrative systems.

3. Disable Unused Services and Ports

• Reduce Network Exposure: Disable any unused network services or close unnecessary ports that are not essential for the system's operation. This reduces the number of access points an attacker can exploit.

o Example: Closing unused ports on a web server to prevent unauthorised access through unused protocols.

• Harden System Configurations: Review default system configurations, which may include unnecessary services, protocols, or network settings. Unused services should be disabled to minimise exposure.

o Example: Disabling Remote Desktop Protocol (RDP) if the system does not require it.

Benefits of Attack Surface Reduction

• Reduced Risk of Exploitation: Minimizing the number of vulnerable points in a system reduces the chances of an attacker finding an exploitable weakness.
• Improved System Resilience: A smaller attack surface means that even if part of the system is compromised, the damage can be limited, and recovery is faster.
• Easier Maintenance: With fewer components and services to manage, updating, patching, and auditing the system becomes easier, leading to better long-term security management.

3.5 Vulnerability Assessment

A vulnerability assessment is a systematic process of identifying, evaluating, and prioritising security vulnerabilities within an information system or application. The primary goal of a vulnerability assessment is to identify weaknesses that attackers could exploit, enabling organisations to address these vulnerabilities before they are compromised.
Vulnerability assessments are essential for maintaining strong security postures for individual applications and entire IT infrastructures. They help organisations identify potential risk areas, understand the severity of identified vulnerabilities, and implement mitigation strategies.

Why Conduct a Vulnerability Assessment?

Vulnerability assessments are critical for maintaining the security and integrity of systems. They help:
• Identify Potential Entry Points: Vulnerabilities often represent entry points attackers can exploit to gain unauthorised access.
• Prioritize Risks: Not all vulnerabilities are equally dangerous. A vulnerability assessment helps prioritise which weaknesses to address based on their severity and the potential damage they could cause.
• Proactively Mitigate Threats: Regular assessments ensure that vulnerabilities are addressed before malicious actors can exploit them.
• Comply with Regulations: Many regulatory frameworks (e.g., PCI DSS, HIPAA) require regular vulnerability assessments for compliance efforts.

Types of Vulnerabilities Assessed

1. Network Vulnerabilities

These vulnerabilities relate to the network infrastructure and can include misconfigurations, open ports, insecure network protocols, or exposed services.
Example: An open port that allows external access to an internal server.

2. System Vulnerabilities

System-level vulnerabilities pertain to the operating systems, hardware, and firmware. They include outdated patches, weak configurations, or insecure default settings.
Example: An unpatched operating system vulnerable to a known exploit.

3. Application Vulnerabilities

These vulnerabilities, including SQL injection, cross-site scripting (XSS), and improper authentication or session management, occur at the application layer.
Example: A web application that allows SQL queries to be injected via a user input field.

4. Configuration Vulnerabilities

Configuration vulnerabilities arise from improper system, application, or network settings. Misconfigurations often create unintended exposures that can be exploited.
Example: An application with verbose error messages that reveal sensitive information about the system's architecture.

5. Human Vulnerabilities

This includes vulnerabilities related to human error, such as weak password policies, social engineering risks, or a lack of security awareness training.
Example: An employee using weak or reused passwords across multiple systems.

Vulnerability Assessment Process

1. Planning

• The planning phase involves defining the scope of the assessment. It determines which systems, networks, and applications will be assessed and the rules of engagement.
• Key Considerations:
What is the scope (e.g., internal, external, network, application)?
Are there any exclusions or limitations?
What tools and techniques will be used?

2. Discovery

• During discovery, assessors gather information about the target environment. This phase involves mapping the network, identifying assets, and discovering services and applications.
Key Activities:
Network scanning to detect active devices and services.
Asset inventory to identify all systems, applications, and devices.
Open port scanning to identify exposed services.

3. Vulnerability Scanning

• Automated tools scan systems, networks, and applications for known vulnerabilities. These tools compare configurations and services against known database weaknesses.
Key Tools:
Network scanners (e.g., Nessus, OpenVAS).
Web application vulnerability scanners (e.g., OWASP ZAP, Burp Suite).
System configuration checkers.

4. Vulnerability Analysis

• Once vulnerabilities are identified, the next step is to analyse their impact and likelihood of exploitation. This phase helps determine which vulnerabilities pose the highest risk to the organisation.
Key Considerations:
Severity of vulnerabilities (e.g., based on CVSS scores).
Exposure level (e.g., externally accessible vs. internal-only).
Potential impact if exploited (e.g., Data loss, service disruption).

5. Risk Evaluation and Prioritization

• Not all vulnerabilities require immediate attention. In this phase, vulnerabilities are categorised based on risk level, helping organisations prioritise remediation efforts.
Key Criteria:
Exploitability: How easy is it to exploit the vulnerability?
Impact: What is the potential damage if the vulnerability is exploited?
Exposure: Is the vulnerability exposed to the public internet or only accessible internally?

Common Vulnerability Assessment Tools

1. Nessus: One of the most widely used network vulnerability scanners, Nessus identifies misconfigurations, open ports, and known vulnerabilities in systems and applications.
2. OpenVAS: An open-source vulnerability scanning tool that performs extensive checks for vulnerabilities and generates reports with remediation recommendations.
3. OWASP ZAP: A web application security scanner that identifies common vulnerabilities like SQL injection, XSS, and security misconfigurations.
4. Burp Suite is a popular tool for web application vulnerability assessments. It identifies issues such as input validation flaws and insecure session handling.
5. QualysGuard is a cloud-based vulnerability management tool that scans systems for vulnerabilities, provides risk assessments, and helps track remediation efforts.

3.6 Defensive Software Architecture

Defensive software architecture is a software design and development approach that emphasises building systems with security in mind from the ground up. The primary goal is to anticipate potential threats and attacks and structure the software to limit the impact of vulnerabilities and mitigate risks. It includes techniques and design principles that create systems that defend themselves against malicious actions, unauthorised access, and other potential compromises.

Defensive architecture involves security best practices at multiple levels, including application, system, and infrastructure design. It ensures that vulnerabilities are difficult to exploit and that the impact of any breach is minimised.

Key Principles of Defensive Software Architecture

1. Defence in Depth

Defense in depth is a layered security strategy where multiple security controls are implemented throughout the system. Even if one layer is breached, others remain to protect the system.

Example: A web application might have input validation, firewall protection, encryption, and user authentication mechanisms, each layer providing additional security.

2. Least Privilege

The principle of least privilege (PoLP) ensures that users, processes, and applications have only the minimum permissions necessary to perform their tasks. This limits the potential damage if credentials or services are compromised.
Example: A Database administrator should have full access to manage the Database, but a general user should only be able to read certain Data, not modify it.

3. Fail-Secure (Fail-Safe)

Systems should be designed to fail securely, meaning that if a failure occurs, the system defaults to a secure state rather than an exposed or vulnerable one.
Example: Access should be denied by default rather than granted if an error occurs during user authentication.

4. Minimize Attack Surface

Reducing the attack surface involves limiting the number of possible entry points for attackers. This can be achieved by disabling unnecessary features, reducing complexity, and removing redundant or deprecated code.
Example: Disabling unused network services and ports reduces the attack vectors available to an attacker.

5. Secure Defaults

Software and systems should be configured with secure defaults. This means that out-of-the-box settings should prioritise security over convenience, ensuring that systems are not left vulnerable due to poor default configurations.
Example: An application should enforce strong password policies by default and require HTTPS for all connections.

6. Segregation of Duties

This principle involves dividing responsibilities and permissions across multiple users or systems to prevent any single control point from having too much power. This reduces the risk of insider threats or compromised accounts, leading to full system control.
Example: Separating the duties of software developers and system administrators so developers do not have full access to production systems.

Strategies for Implementing Defensive Software Architecture

1. Modular and Component-Based Architecture

- A modular architecture divides a system into separate components that interact with each other through well-defined interfaces. This separation ensures that vulnerabilities in one module do not necessarily compromise the entire system.
- Example: A microservices architecture where each service operates independently, with limited communication through APIs.

2. Threat Modeling

- Threat modelling involves identifying potential threats to the system and designing defences to mitigate them. This process occurs early in the development lifecycle and helps identify possible attack vectors before they become real vulnerabilities.
- Example: Identifying that a web application might be susceptible to SQL injection and designing input validation techniques to prevent it.

3. Use of Security Patterns

- Security patterns are proven solutions for common security problems. These patterns give developers reusable security practices to implement across different system parts.
- Examples of Common Security Patterns:

  Authentication and Authorization: Using tokens or OAuth for secure identity management.

  Encrypted Data Storage: Applying encryption patterns to protect sensitive data at rest.

4. Encryption and Secure Communication

- Encryption is crucial for protecting sensitive Data both in transit and at rest. Ensuring that all sensitive communications use robust encryption algorithms protects against interception and tampering.
- Example: Using TLS (Transport Layer Security) to encrypt communications between a client and a server.

5. Continuous Security Testing

- Security testing is not a one-time activity. Continuous integration and delivery pipelines should include automated security testing, such as static code analysis, penetration testing, and vulnerability scanning.
- Example: Running regular automated tests to detect vulnerabilities like SQL injection, buffer overflow, or cross-site scripting.

3.7 Glossary

1. Cookies and Session Headers

- Cookies: The web browser stores Small pieces of Data on a user's device. Used to maintain stateful information (e.g., session IDs) across multiple pages.

• Session: A series of interactions between a user and a web application, typically maintained by session cookies or tokens.
• Session Headers: HTTP headers are used to pass session-related information between the client and server.

2. OWASP Top 10 Flaws

• OWASP Top 10: A list of the ten most critical web application security risks, as identified by the Open Web Application Security Project (OWASP). Examples include injection, broken authentication, and cross-site scripting (XSS).
• Injection Attacks: A security vulnerability where an attacker can insert malicious code (e.g., SQL, commands) into a web application's input fields.
• Cross-Site Scripting (XSS): A vulnerability that allows attackers to inject malicious scripts into web pages viewed by other users.

3. Security Fundamentals: Input Validation

• Input Validation ensures that user-provided Data is safe, well-formed, and free from harmful content before it is processed.
• Whitelist Validation: A type of input validation where only predefined, safe Data is accepted.
• Sanitization: Modifying or filtering user input to remove or neutralise potentially harmful elements.

Attack Surface Reduction

• Attack Surface: The total number of entry points where an attacker can attempt to exploit vulnerabilities in a system.
• Attack Surface Reduction: The process of minimising potential attack vectors by disabling unnecessary services, limiting exposed APIs, and closing unused ports.

4. Vulnerability Assessment

• Vulnerability: A weakness or flaw in a system that can be exploited by attackers.
• Vulnerability Assessment: The process of identifying, classifying, and prioritising vulnerabilities in a system, often through automated tools or manual testing.

5. Defensive Software Architecture

• Defensive Software Architecture: A software design approach that emphasises security from the ground up, implementing multiple layers of protection and minimising vulnerabilities.
• Defense in Depth: A layered security strategy that uses multiple defensive measures to protect the system even if one layer is compromised.
• Least Privilege: A security principle that ensures users and applications have the minimum access necessary to perform their tasks.

6. Comprehensive Code Reviews

• Code Review: A systematic code examination by developers to identify errors, vulnerabilities, and areas for improvement before merging code into a codebase.
• Static Code Analysis: Automated tools that analyse source code for errors, security vulnerabilities, and coding standards violations without executing the program.
• Security Review: This is a part of the code review process focused specifically on identifying potential security issues in the code.

3.8 Summary

This glossary highlights critical terms and concepts related to web application security and defensive software development, breaking down essential topics covered in the broader chapters.

• Web Application Security refers to protecting web applications from various threats and vulnerabilities, including unauthorised access and Data breaches. Key techniques include secure coding, robust authentication, and Data encryption.

• Cookies and Session Headers: Cookies store user session Data on the client side, while session headers manage communication between client and server during a user's interaction with a web application. Securing these mechanisms prevents session hijacking and other threats.

• OWASP Top 10 Flaws: A widely recognised list of web applications' most critical security risks. It includes vulnerabilities like injection attacks, broken authentication, and cross-site scripting (XSS), which can be exploited to compromise systems.

• Security Fundamentals: Input Validation: Input validation ensures that user-provided Data is properly checked before processing, helping prevent security issues like injection attacks. Whitelist validation and sanitisation are key techniques to secure inputs.

• Attack Surface Reduction: Reducing the attack surface involves minimising the number of entry points or exposed services that attackers could exploit, thereby making the system more secure.
• Vulnerability Assessment: A process of identifying and assessing security weaknesses in a system, often using both automated tools and manual techniques to prioritise and address risks before they are exploited.
• Defensive Software Architecture: This approach involves building security into the software design, using principles like defence in depth, least privilege, and secure defaults. It focuses on proactively minimising the impact of vulnerabilities.
• Comprehensive Code Reviews: A key step in the software development process, code reviews help detect errors, improve code quality, and ensure the code is secure. These reviews check for functionality, performance, security, and maintainability.

3.9 Previous Year Solved Questions

Question. What are the core components of web application security, and how do defensive software architecture principles, comprehensive code reviews, and input validation contribute to creating a secure and resilient application? (Delhi University, 2023 MCA)

Answer. Web application security is a multifaceted discipline that protects applications from various threats and vulnerabilities. Its core components include secure coding practices, robust authentication and authorisation mechanisms, Data encryption, and proactive threat detection. Critical practices such as defensive software architecture, comprehensive code reviews, and rigorous input validation play crucial roles in ensuring an application's security and resilience.

Defensive Software Architecture is a proactive approach to designing software with built-in security features. It involves principles such as:

• **Defense in Depth:** Implementing multiple layers of security controls to protect the system, so if one layer is breached, others continue to offer protection.
• **Least Privilege:** Ensuring that users, processes, and applications have only the minimum level of access necessary for their functions, reducing the potential impact of a compromise.
• **Fail-Secure:** Designing systems to fail securely, defaulting to a state of minimal risk if a failure occurs.
• **Secure by Design:** Integrating security considerations into the design phase to prevent vulnerabilities from being introduced later in development.

These principles help create a robust architecture that anticipates potential threats and mitigates risks effectively.

Comprehensive Code Reviews are a critical process in maintaining high-quality and secure code. They involve systematic examination by peers or automated tools to identify issues such as:

• **Functionality and Correctness:** Ensuring the code meets functional requirements and appropriately handles edge cases.
• **Security Vulnerabilities:** Checking for common security risks such as injection attacks, cross-site scripting (XSS), and improper access controls.
• **Performance and Efficiency:** Identifying performance bottlenecks and optimising the code for speed and resource usage.
• **Readability and Maintainability:** Verifying that the code is well-documented, adheres to coding standards, and is easy to understand and modify.

Code reviews help prevent bugs and vulnerabilities from entering production by catching issues early, thereby improving the application's overall security posture.

Input validation is a fundamental practice that protects web applications from malicious inputs. It involves:

• **Validating User Inputs:** Ensuring that Data submitted by users is checked for correctness and safety before processing helps prevent injection attacks and Data corruption.
• **Whitelist Validation:** Accepting only predefined, safe inputs while rejecting anything that doesn't match expected patterns.
• **Sanitization:** Modifying or filtering inputs to remove or neutralise potentially harmful content, ensuring that outputs are safe for users and systems.

Effective input validation prevents attackers from exploiting vulnerabilities through manipulated or unexpected Data, protecting the application from various security threats.

In summary, web application security requires a comprehensive approach integrating defensive software architecture principles, rigorous code reviews, and robust input validation. These practices collectively create secure, resilient applications that are better protected against threats and vulnerabilities. By adopting these strategies, organisations can ensure that their web applications are safe, maintainable, and capable of withstanding potential attacks.

Exercises

Exercise 1 – Multiple Choice Questions

1. What is the OWASP Top 10?
a) A list of web application security risks
b) A list of the top 10 programming languages
c) A standard for web application design
d) A type of input validation method

2. Which of the following is a technique used to reduce the attack surface?
a) Code Review
b) Attack Surface Reduction
c) Cross-Site Scripting (XSS)
d) Session Hijacking

Exercise 2 – True/False

1. Cookies are used to store user session Data on the client side. (True/False)
2. Cross-Site Scripting (XSS) is a technique used to validate user inputs. (True/False)

Exercise 3 – Fill in the blanks

1. __________ refers to the process of ensuring user-provided Data is safe and free from harmful content.
2. The principle of __________ ensures that users and applications have the minimum level of access necessary to perform their tasks.

Exercise 4- Fill in the blanks with two options

1. __________ and __________ are techniques used to ensure input Data is safe before processing.
2. The __________ approach to software design involves implementing multiple layers of protection.

Exercise 5- Rearrange the sentence

1. Validation / Input / ensures / user-provided / Data / is / safe / before / processing
2. Cookies / store / on / client-side / Data / user-session

Exercise 6- Choose the Odd One Out

1. a) SQL Injection
b) Cross-Site Scripting (XSS)
c) Session Hijacking
d) Static Code Analysis

2. a) Least Privilege
b) Defence in Depth
c) Attack Surface Reduction
d) Injection Attacks

Exercise 7- Jumble words

1. EVCADILTAON
2. TROSECUTI

Exercise 8- Match case

1. Cookies
2. OWASP Top 10
3. Input Validation
4. Session Headers

a) HTTP headers used to pass session-related information
b) List of critical web application security risks

c) Small pieces of Data stored on a user's device
d) Ensuring Data is safe and free from harmful content

Exercise 9- Assertion – Reason

1. Assertion: Input validation is critical for preventing injection attacks.
Reason: It ensures that user-provided Data is safe and well-formed.
a) Both Assertion and Reason are correct and Reason is the correct explanation for Assertion.
b) Both Assertion and Reason are correct but Reason is not the correct explanation for Assertion.
c) Assertion is correct but Reason is incorrect.
d) Assertion is incorrect but Reason is correct.

2. Assertion: Defensive software architecture focuses on secure coding practices.
Reason: It involves implementing multiple layers of protection and minimizing vulnerabilities.
a) Both Assertion and Reason are correct and Reason is the correct explanation for Assertion.
b) Both Assertion and Reason are correct but Reason is not the correct explanation for Assertion.
c) Assertion is correct but Reason is incorrect.
d) Assertion is incorrect but Reason is correct.

Exercise 10- Read the questions given below and find the appropriate word in the grid provided.

Questions:

1. The protection of web applications from unauthorized access and Data breaches, including secure coding and Data encryption, is referred to as __________.
2. The OWASP Top 10 Flaws include vulnerabilities like injection attacks and cross-site scripting (XSS). This list is recognized for identifying the most critical __________ to web applications.

Grid:

M	H	O	A	I	J	B	J	Q	N	H	C
W	E	B	A	P	P	S	C	R	I	T	Y
M	K	E	P	O	P	V	N	M	P	H	E
T	A	I	S	N	E	S	S	N	O	R	R
A	R	P	S	P	O	O	F	I	N	W	G
T	M	N	O	S	A	F	L	H	K	V	A
T	Q	W	O	T	R	C	A	G	W	G	L
A	W	D	F	N	B	T	W	U	Z	X	K
C	V	B	I	W	F	B	S	A	X	Z	J
K	H	I	V	Y	J	K	K	D	C	E	M

.Exercise 11- One- word

1. What term is used for the practice of reviewing code to find and fix vulnerabilities?
2. What is the term for the security measure that limits user access to the minimum necessary for their role?

Exercise 12- Small Answers

1. What is the purpose of session headers in web application security?
2. Explain "Whitelist Validation."

Exercise 13- Long Answers

1. Describe the OWASP Top 10 Flaws and their impact on web application security.
2. Explain the concept of Defensive Software Architecture and its importance in web application security.

Exercise 14- Previous Year Unsolved Questions

1. Discuss the conditions under which a person is liable to pay damages for violating the provisions of the Information Technology Act, 2000. (IGNOU, 2022 MCA)
2. ''Authentication is one of the most important of all information security objectives.'' Critically examine the statement. (IGNOU, 2022 MCA)
3. (a) Explain any five security issues in cyberspace.
(b) What are the three governing principles of Data security? Explain how these three principles can be implemented.
(c) Explain any two strategies of regulating the Internet.
(d) What is the meaning of Intellectual Property? Explain the following forms of intellectual property:
a) Copyright and related rights
b) Patents (IGNOU, June 2023, MCA)
4. (a) How can technology be used to answer the following security issues?
a) Unauthorized access
b) Malwares
c) Phishing
(b) What is the use of cryptography? Explain the concept of substitution cipher with the help of an example. (IGNOU, June 2023, MCA)
5. (a) Explain the concept and uses of digital signature and digital certificates.
(b) Explain the following terms:
a) Security audit
b) Security policy (IGNOU, June 2023, MCA)
6. (a) What is the purpose of using filtering devices and rating system on the Internet? Discuss the offenses in the context of regulation of cyber law content in India.
(b) List the four categories of cyber crimes. List various cyber crimes of each category. How is cyber crime different from traditional crime? (IGNOU, June 2023, MCA)
7. (a) What do you understand by DOS and DDOS attack? Explain in detail.
(b) Write a note on intellectual property aspects in cyber laws. (Mumbai University, December 2023, MCA)
8. (a) Explain SQL injection attack.
b) Explain Objectives and features of IT Act 2000. (Mumbai University, December 2023, MCA)

Answers

Exercise 1- 1. a) A list of web application security risks, 2. b) Attack Surface Reduction
Exercise 2- 1.True, 2. False
Exercise 3- 1.Input Validation, 2.Least Privilege
Exercise 4- 1.Whitelist Validation and Sanitization, 2. Defensive
Exercise 5- 1. Input validation ensures user-provided Data is safe before processing, 2. Cookies store user-session Data on client-side
Exercise 6- 1. d) Static Code Analysis, 2. d) Injection Attacks
Exercise 7- 1. VALIDATION, 2. SECURE
Exercise 8- 1- c, 2 – b, 3 – 4 - a
Exercise 9- 1. True, 2. True
Exercise 10- 1. WEB APP SECURITY, 2. FLAWS

M	H	O	A	I	J	B	J	Q	N	H	C
W	E	B	A	P	P	S	C	R	I	T	Y
M	K	E	P	O	P	V	N	M	P	H	E
T	A	I	S	N	E	S	S	N	O	R	R
A	M	L	S	P	O	O	F	I	N	W	G
T	M	N	O	S	A	F	L	H	K	V	A
T	Q	W	O	T	R	C	A	G	W	G	L
A	W	D	F	N	B	T	W	U	Z	X	K
C	V	B	I	W	F	B	S	A	X	Z	J
K	H	I	V	Y	J	K	K	D	C	E	M

Exercise 11- 1. Code Review, 2. Least Privilege

Test Paper

Chapter-3

Web Application Security

Time Duration: 30 Minutes **Maximum Marks: 25**

General Instructions:

1. The question paper consists of 12 questions and is divided into four sections, A, B, C and D.
2. All questions are compulsory.
3. Section A comprises MCQs, Fill in the blanks and True or False carrying one marks each.
4. Section B comprises VSAQs(very short answers questions) carrying two marks each.
5. Section C comprises SAQs(short questions) carrying four marks each.
6. Section D comprises long questions carrying five marks each.

SECTION-A

I. Multiple choice questions: **(1*2=2)**

1. What is the OWASP Top 10?

a. A list of the ten most critical web application security risks
b. A guide to secure coding practices
c. A software for vulnerability assessment
d. A firewall configuration standard

2. Which of the following is a method to minimize the attack surface of a web application?

a. Using static code analysis tools
b. Implementing least privilege access
c. Regular password changes
d. Encrypting all Data at rest

II. Fill in the blanks: **(1*2=2)**

1. __________ involves a systematic review of code to find errors and vulnerabilities before merging it into a codebase.
2. __________ refers to a vulnerability where an attacker can inject malicious scripts into web pages viewed by other users.

I. True or False: **(1*2=2)**

1. Input validation helps in preventing injection attacks by ensuring that user Data is properly checked.
2. Cookies are used to store session-related information on the server side.

SECTION-B

IV. Very Short answers type questions- **(2*3=6)**

1. Define Cross-Site Scripting (XSS).
2. What is the purpose of session headers in web applications?
3. Explain the term "Attack Surface Reduction".

SECTION-C

V. Short answers type questions-I **(4*2=8)**

1. Describe the role of input validation in web application security.
2. Compare WPA2 and WPA3 in terms of security features.

SECTION-D

VI. Long answers type questions **(5*1=5)**

1. Discuss the importance of defensive software architecture in securing web applications. Include concepts such as Defense in Depth and Least Privilege in your discussion.

ONLINE RESOURCES

Practice Paper
Link: https://forms.gle/p22n5qPaTfsQAyjU9
QR Code:

YouTube Video Playlist Link
Link: https://www.youtube.com/playlist?list=PLzlh_31VWEFoQmknN6oEeZarlNzsUELrh
QR Code:

Chapter 4 - Vulnerability Management

In this chapter you will learn about:

Vulnerability Discovery: Techniques and Tools
Vulnerability Regression Testing
Responsible Disclosure Programs
Vulnerability Analysis and Ranking
Common Vulnerability Scoring System (CVSS)
Advanced Vulnerability Scoring

In the realm of cybersecurity, vulnerability management is a critical process aimed at identifying, assessing, prioritizing, and mitigating vulnerabilities in systems, applications, and networks. The goal is to minimize the risk posed by these vulnerabilities, thereby protecting an organization's assets, Data, and reputation.

What is Vulnerability Management?

Vulnerability management is an ongoing, systematic approach to discovering, analyzing, and addressing security weaknesses that could be exploited by attackers. It involves several key activities:

1. Identification: Detecting vulnerabilities through various means, including automated scanning tools, manual testing, and threat intelligence.
2. Assessment: Evaluating the severity and potential impact of identified vulnerabilities to determine their risk level.
3. Prioritization: Ranking vulnerabilities based on their risk, exploitability, and impact on the organization to focus resources on the most critical issues.
4. Remediation: Applying patches, updates, or other fixes to address vulnerabilities and mitigate their potential risks.
5. Verification: Ensuring that the applied fixes effectively resolve the vulnerabilities and do not introduce new issues.
6. Monitoring: Continuously tracking the security environment for new vulnerabilities and assessing the effectiveness of the vulnerability management process.

4.1 Vulnerability Discovery: Techniques and Tools

Vulnerability discovery is a crucial phase in the vulnerability management process. It involves identifying potential security weaknesses that could be exploited by attackers. This section explores various techniques and tools used to discover vulnerabilities in systems, applications, and networks.

Techniques for Vulnerability Discovery

1. Automated Scanning

a. **Description**: Automated scanning tools systematically search for known vulnerabilities in systems, applications, and networks. These tools compare the system's configuration against a Database of known vulnerabilities and security issues.

b. **Examples**:

Network Scanners: Tools like Nessus and OpenVAS scan network devices and services for vulnerabilities.

Web Application Scanners: Tools like OWASP ZAP and Burp Suite assess web applications for common vulnerabilities like XSS and SQL injection.

2. Manual Testing

a. **Description**: Manual testing involves skilled security professionals conducting detailed examinations of systems and applications to discover vulnerabilities that automated tools might miss.

b. **Examples**:

Penetration Testing: Ethical hackers simulate attacks to identify security weaknesses. Techniques include social engineering, exploiting known vulnerabilities, and probing for misconfigurations.

Code Reviews: Security experts review source code to identify potential security flaws, such as improper handling of user inputs or insecure coding practices.

3. Threat Intelligence

a. **Description**: Threat intelligence involves gathering and analyzing information about emerging threats and vulnerabilities from various sources, such as security advisories, vendor updates, and threat feeds.

b. **Examples**:

Security Advisories: Information from organizations like CERT and vendor security bulletins about newly discovered vulnerabilities.

Threat Feeds: Real-time Data on emerging threats and exploits that can help in identifying vulnerabilities in your environment.

4. Configuration Review

a. Description: This technique involves reviewing system and application configurations to ensure they adhere to security best practices and do not expose vulnerabilities due to misconfiguration.

b. Examples:

System Hardening: Ensuring that systems are configured securely by disabling unnecessary services, closing unused ports, and applying security settings.

Application Configurations: Checking application settings to ensure they do not expose sensitive Data or create security risks.

5. Fuzz Testing

a. Description: Fuzz testing involves inputting random, unexpected, or malformed Data into a system to uncover vulnerabilities such as crashes or unexpected behaviours.

b. Examples:

Fuzzers: Tools like AFL (American Fuzzy Lop) and Peach Fuzzer generate and test a wide range of inputs to find software vulnerabilities.

Tools for Vulnerability Discovery

1. Nessus

Description: A widely used network vulnerability scanner that identifies vulnerabilities, misconfigurations, and compliance issues across networked systems.

Features: Comprehensive vulnerability checks, customisable scanning policies, and detailed reporting.

2. OWASP ZAP (Zed Attack Proxy)

Description: An open-source web application security scanner designed to find vulnerabilities in web applications.

Features: Automated scanners, passive scanning, and powerful add-ons for advanced testing.

3. Burp Suite

Description: A popular web application security testing tool that provides features for crawling, scanning, and analysing web applications for security vulnerabilities.

Features: Intercepting proxy, automated vulnerability scanner, and extensive plugin support.

4. OpenVAS

Description: An open-source vulnerability scanner that comprehensively assesses network security vulnerabilities.

Features: Regularly updated vulnerability Database, customisable scanning options, and detailed reporting.

5. AFL (American Fuzzy Lop)

Description: A fuzzer used for discovering vulnerabilities by generating many random inputs to test software for crashes and unexpected behaviours.

Features: High-performance fuzzing, easy setup, and effective finding subtle bugs.

4.2 Vulnerability Regression Testing

Vulnerability regression testing is a critical process in the vulnerability management lifecycle that verifies that previously identified and fixed vulnerabilities do not reappear in the system after remediation efforts. This type of testing ensures that security fixes are effective and that new changes do not introduce previously resolved issues.

What is Vulnerability Regression Testing?

Vulnerability regression testing is a testing process to confirm that vulnerabilities previously identified and patched remain fixed after updates, changes, or new code deployments. It ensures that remediation efforts are sustained and new vulnerabilities have not been introduced inadvertently.

Why is Vulnerability Regression Testing Important?

1. Validation of Fixes: It verifies that patches and fixes applied to address vulnerabilities continue to work as intended and that the vulnerabilities do not reappear.

2. Prevention of Regressions: It helps prevent the recurrence of security issues that were previously resolved, ensuring that fixes are effective across system updates and changes.

3. Consistency in Security Posture: Ensures that new code or system changes do not undermine the security measures already in place, maintaining a consistent security posture.

4. Compliance and Risk Management: Helps meet regulatory and compliance requirements by demonstrating that vulnerabilities are managed effectively over time.

Techniques for Vulnerability Regression Testing

1. Re-running Automated Scans

Description: Automated vulnerability scanning tools are re-run after fixes or updates to ensure that previously identified vulnerabilities have been effectively resolved and no new issues have been introduced.

Benefits: Provides a quick and comprehensive assessment of the system's security status.

Tools: Nessus, OpenVAS, and Qualys.

2. Manual Verification

Description: Security experts manually verify that vulnerabilities have been fixed by reproducing the conditions under which the vulnerabilities were previously exploited.

Benefits: Allows for detailed validation and can identify issues that automated tools might miss.

Methods: Penetration testing and code reviews.

3. Regression Testing Suites

Description: Testing suites designed to check that previously fixed vulnerabilities remain addressed in the context of new code changes or system updates.

Benefits: Ensures the overall application or system functionality remains secure after updates.

Components: Unit tests, integration tests, and end-to-end tests.

4. Patch Management Verification

Description: Ensures that patches applied to fix vulnerabilities are still effective by verifying that the patch is implemented correctly and has not been bypassed or undone.

Benefits: Confirms that patches are integrated correctly and do not introduce new issues.

Processes: Patch deployment verification and testing.

4. Continuous Integration/Continuous Deployment (CI/CD) Integration

Description: Integrates vulnerability regression testing into the CI/CD pipeline to automatically test for vulnerabilities as part of the build and deployment process.

Benefits: Provides ongoing assurance that vulnerabilities are managed throughout the development lifecycle.

Tools: Jenkins, GitLab CI, and Azure DevOps.

4.3 Responsible Disclosure Programs

Responsible disclosure programs are initiatives designed to encourage reporting security vulnerabilities in a manner that protects both the security researcher and the organisation affected by the vulnerability. These programs create a structured framework for reporting, assessing, and addressing vulnerabilities, promoting collaboration between security researchers and organisations to enhance overall security.

What is a Responsible Disclosure Program?

A responsible disclosure program is a structured process that allows security researchers, ethical hackers, and other individuals to report discovered vulnerabilities safely and responsibly. It includes guidelines and protocols for reporting, handling, and resolving vulnerabilities to address security issues effectively while minimising potential risks to users and systems.

Why are Responsible Disclosure Programs Important?

1. Enhanced Security: By encouraging the reporting of vulnerabilities, organisations can address and mitigate potential security issues before they are exploited by malicious actors.

2. Collaboration: These programs foster a collaborative environment between security researchers and organizations, facilitating knowledge sharing and improving security practices.

3. Reputation Management: Responsible vulnerability management helps maintain the organization's reputation and demonstrates a commitment to security and transparency.

4. Legal Protection: Responsible disclosure programs provide legal protections for researchers, ensuring they are not subjected to legal action for their efforts in identifying and reporting vulnerabilities.

Key Components of a Responsible Disclosure Program

1. Disclosure Policy

Description: A formal policy outlining how vulnerabilities should be reported, what information is needed, and the process for handling reports.

Elements: Contact details, reporting guidelines, response times, and legal protections for researchers.

2. Reporting Channels

Description: Secure and confidential methods for submitting vulnerability reports.

Examples: Dedicated email addresses, web forms, or bug bounty platforms.

Best Practices: Ensure secure communication to protect sensitive information.

3. Vulnerability Assessment
Description: Evaluate reported vulnerabilities' severity, impact, and validity.
Steps: Verify the vulnerability, assess the potential impact, and prioritise remediation.
4. Remediation Process
Description: The steps taken to address and fix reported vulnerabilities.
Components: Development of patches or updates, testing of fixes, and deployment of solutions.
Communication: Regular updates to the researcher on the status of the reported issue.

4.4 Vulnerability Analysis and Ranking

Vulnerability analysis and ranking are crucial components of an effective vulnerability management program. This process involves evaluating identified vulnerabilities to determine their severity, potential impact, and priority for remediation. Organisations can allocate resources efficiently by systematically analysing and ranking vulnerabilities and addressing the most critical issues first.

What is Vulnerability Analysis and Ranking?

Vulnerability analysis examines and understands the nature, impact, and exploitability of vulnerabilities discovered in a system, application, or network. Ranking involves assigning a priority or severity level to each vulnerability based on its characteristics and potential impact. This helps organisations focus on the most significant threats and manage their security posture effectively.

Why is Vulnerability Analysis and Ranking Important?

1. **Resource Allocation:** Prioritizing vulnerabilities ensures that limited resources are used effectively to address the most critical issues first.
2. **Risk Management:** This helps manage and mitigate risks by focusing on vulnerabilities that pose the highest threat to the organization.
3. **Compliance:** Many regulations and standards require organisations to assess and prioritise vulnerabilities as part of their security management practices.
4. **Incident Prevention:** By addressing high-priority vulnerabilities promptly, organisations can prevent potential security incidents and breaches.

Key Components of Vulnerability Analysis and Ranking

1. Vulnerability Assessment

a. **Description**: The process of evaluating the characteristics of identified vulnerabilities to understand their nature and potential impact.

b. **Steps**:

Identification: Determine the specific details of the vulnerability, such as affected systems, software versions, and potential exploit vectors.

Analysis: Assess the vulnerability's potential impact on the organisation, including the possible consequences of an exploit.

2. Severity Scoring

a. **Description**: Assigning a numerical score or qualitative rating to vulnerabilities based on their severity and potential impact.

b. **Systems**:

CVSS (Common Vulnerability Scoring System): A widely used system that provides a standardised score for vulnerabilities based on factors such as exploitability, impact, and complexity.

Risk Matrix: A framework that evaluates vulnerabilities based on their likelihood and potential impact, often using a scale from low to high.

3. Impact Analysis

a. **Description**: Evaluating the potential consequences of exploiting a vulnerability, including Data loss, system downtime, financial loss, and reputational damage.

b. **Factors**:

Data Sensitivity: The type and sensitivity of Data at risk.

System Criticality: The importance of the affected system or application to business operations.

Exposure: The likelihood of the vulnerability being exploited, considering factors such as network exposure and access controls.

4.5 Common Vulnerability Scoring System (CVSS)

The Common Vulnerability Scoring System (CVSS) is a standardized framework for assessing and quantifying the severity of vulnerabilities in software and systems. It provides a consistent method for evaluating the impact and exploitability of vulnerabilities, allowing organisations to prioritise their response and remediation efforts effectively.

What is CVSS?

CVSS is an open standard for measuring the severity of vulnerabilities. Developed by the National Vulnerability Database (NVD) and maintained by the Forum of Incident Response and Security Teams (FIRST), it provides a numerical score that reflects a vulnerability's potential impact and helps organizations assess its criticality.

Why is CVSS Important?

1. Standardization: CVSS provides a consistent and widely accepted method for scoring vulnerabilities, making it easier to compare and prioritise issues across different systems and organisations.
2. Prioritization: By assigning vulnerabilities a severity score, CVSS helps organizations prioritize remediation efforts based on each vulnerability's potential impact and exploitability.
3. Communication: CVSS scores facilitate clear communication about the severity of vulnerabilities between security teams, management, and other stakeholders.
4. Risk Management: CVSS scores contribute to risk management by quantitatively measuring vulnerability severity, aiding in decision-making and resource allocation.

CVSS Metrics

CVSS scores are derived from several metrics that assess different aspects of a vulnerability. The system consists of three metric groups: Base, Temporal, and Environmental.

1. Base Metrics

o Description: These metrics represent the intrinsic characteristics of a vulnerability that remain constant over time and across different environments.

o Components:

• Attack Vector (AV): Indicates how the vulnerability is exploited, such as locally, remotely, or physically.
• Options: Network (N), Adjacent Network (A), Local (L), Physical (P)
• Attack Complexity (AC): Describes the complexity of the attack required to exploit the vulnerability.
• Options: Low (L), High (H)
• Privileges Required (PR): Specifies the level of access an attacker needs before exploiting the vulnerability.
• Options: None (N), Low (L), High (H)
• User Interaction (UI): Indicates whether user interaction is required to exploit the vulnerability.
• Options: None (N), Required (R)
• Scope (S): This indicates whether the vulnerability's exploitation affects only the vulnerable component or has a wider impact.
• Options: Unchanged (U), Changed (C)
• Confidentiality Impact (C): Measures the impact on the confidentiality of the affected system or Data.
• Options: None (N), Low (L), High (H)
• Integrity Impact (I): Measures the impact on the integrity of the affected system or Data.
• Options: None (N), Low (L), High (H)
• Availability Impact (A): Measures the impact on the availability of the affected system or Data.
• Options: None (N), Low (L), High (H)

2. Temporal Metrics

o Description: These metrics represent vulnerability characteristics that may change over time, such as the availability of an exploit or the effectiveness of mitigations.

o Components:

• Exploit Code Maturity (E): Indicates the availability of exploit code for the vulnerability.
• Options: Not Defined (X), Unproven (U), Proof-of-Concept (P), Functional (F), High (H)
• Remediation Level (RL): Describes the availability of a fix or workaround for the vulnerability.
• Options: Not Defined (X), Official Fix (O), Temporary Fix (T), Workaround (W), Unavailable (U)
• Report Confidence (RC) reflects the degree of confidence in the vulnerability's existence and impact.
• Options: Not Defined (X), Unknown (U), Reasonable (R), Confirmed (C)

3. Environmental Metrics

o Description: These metrics assess the potential impact of a vulnerability within a specific environment, considering factors such as the affected system's or Data's importance.

o Components:

• Modified Attack Vector (MAV): The attack vector in the specific environment.

• Modified Attack Complexity (MAC): The complexity of the attack in the specific environment.
• Modified Privileges Required (MPR): The level of access required in the specific environment.
• Modified User Interaction (MUI): Whether user interaction is required in the specific environment.
• Modified Scope (MS): The scope of the impact in the specific environment.
• Modified Confidentiality Impact (MC): The confidentiality impact in the specific environment.
• Modified Integrity Impact (MI): The integrity impact in the specific environment.
• Modified Availability Impact (MA): The availability impact in the specific environment.

Calculating CVSS Scores
CVSS scores are calculated based on the values assigned to the Base, Temporal, and Environmental metrics. The base score is calculated first to provide a fundamental measure of the severity of the vulnerability. The Temporal and Environmental scores are then used to adjust the Base score based on factors such as exploitability and the specific context of the vulnerability.
The final CVSS score is a numerical value between 0 and 10, with higher scores indicating more severe vulnerabilities. The score is often presented with a qualitative rating, such as Low, Medium, High, or Critical, to provide a clear and actionable assessment of the severity of the vulnerability.

4.6 Advanced Vulnerability Scoring

Advanced vulnerability scoring methods extend beyond the basic metrics of frameworks like the Common Vulnerability Scoring System (CVSS) to provide more nuanced and context-specific assessments of vulnerabilities. These methods offer deeper insights into vulnerabilities' potential impact and exploitability, allowing organisations to better prioritise and manage their security risks.
What is Advanced Vulnerability Scoring?
Advanced vulnerability scoring refers to enhanced techniques and methodologies for evaluating and ranking vulnerabilities, incorporating additional factors and context-specific information. These methods build upon foundational systems like CVSS, integrating broader considerations such as threat intelligence, exploitability trends, business impact, and dynamic threat landscapes.
Why is Advanced Vulnerability Scoring Important?
1. Contextual Relevance: Provides more tailored assessments of vulnerabilities based on specific organisational contexts and threat environments.
2. Improved Prioritization: Allows for more accurate prioritisation of vulnerabilities by considering factors beyond basic severity, such as business impact and exploit trends.
3. Enhanced Risk Management: Supports more effective risk management by incorporating comprehensive Data and threat intelligence into vulnerability assessments.
4. Dynamic Adaptation: Adapts to evolving threat landscapes and emerging vulnerabilities, ensuring that scoring reflects current and relevant information.

Components of Advanced Vulnerability Scoring
1. Threat Intelligence Integration
Description: Incorporates Data from threat intelligence sources to enhance the understanding of vulnerabilities and their relevance to the organisation.
Sources:
• Threat Feeds: Real-time Data on active threats, exploit techniques, and attacker tactics.
• Security Advisories: Updates from security organisations, vendors, and researchers on emerging threats and vulnerabilities.
Benefits: Provides insight into the likelihood of exploitation and helps prioritise vulnerabilities based on current threat activity.
2. Exploitability Trends
Description: Assesses how trends in exploitability affect the urgency of addressing vulnerabilities.
Factors:
• Exploit Code Availability: Tracks the development and distribution of exploit code for vulnerabilities.
• Exploit Kits: Monitors the use of exploit kits in the wild that target specific vulnerabilities.
Benefits: Helps predict and prioritise vulnerabilities based on the likelihood of exploitation and real-world attack scenarios.
3. Business Impact Analysis

Description: Evaluate the potential impact of a vulnerability on business operations, including financial, operational, and reputational consequences.
Components:
• Asset Criticality: Assesses the importance of affected systems or Data to business operations.
• Operational Impact: Analyzes potential disruptions or downtime resulting from an exploit.
• Reputational Damage: Considers the potential harm to the organisation's reputation and customer trust.
Benefits: Aligns vulnerability prioritisation with business priorities and risk management goals.

4.7 Glossary

• **Advanced Vulnerability Scoring**
A methodology for evaluating and ranking vulnerabilities using enhanced techniques and context-specific information, integrating threat intelligence, exploitability trends, and business impact to improve prioritisation and risk management.
• **Attack Vector (AV)**
A CVSS metric indicates how the vulnerability is exploited, such as network, adjacent network, local, or physical.
• **Attack Complexity (AC)**
A CVSS metric describing the complexity of the attack required to exploit a vulnerability, categorised as low or high.
• **Business Impact Analysis**
Assessment of the potential consequences of a vulnerability on business operations, including financial, operational, and reputational impacts.
• **Common Vulnerability Scoring System (CVSS)**
A standardised framework for assessing and quantifying the severity of vulnerabilities in software and systems, providing a numerical score based on various metrics.
• **Confidentiality Impact (C)**
A CVSS metric measuring the impact on the confidentiality of the affected system or Data, with options for none, low, or high.
• **Dynamic Scoring Adjustments**
Modifying vulnerability scores based on changing conditions, such as new threat intelligence and exploit trends, ensures relevance and accuracy over time.
• **Exploit Code Maturity (E)**
A CVSS temporal metric indicates the availability and maturity of exploit code for a vulnerability, ranging from unproven to high.
• **Exploitability Assessment**
Evaluation of how easily a vulnerability can be exploited, including factors such as the availability of exploit code, required skills, and attack vectors.
• **Exploitability Trends**
Analysis of trends related to the exploitability of vulnerabilities, including the availability of exploit code and the use of exploit kits.
• **Environmental Metrics**
CVSS metrics assess the potential impact of a vulnerability within a specific environment, considering factors such as asset criticality and operational implications.
• **Integrity Impact (I)**
A CVSS metric measuring the impact on the integrity of the affected system or Data, with options for none, low, or high.
• **Modified Attack Vector (MAV)**
An environmental metric that reflects the attack vector in the specific context of the organisation or environment.
• **Modified Attack Complexity (MAC)**
An environmental metric indicates the attack's complexity in the specific context of the organisation or environment.
• **Modified Confidentiality Impact (MC)**
An environmental metric measuring the confidentiality impact of the vulnerability within the specific context of the organisation or environment.
• **Modified Integrity Impact (MI)**
An environmental metric measuring the integrity impact of the vulnerability within the specific context of the organisation or environment.
• **Modified Privileges Required (MPR)**

An environmental metric describing the level of access required in the specific context of the organisation or environment.

• Modified Scope (MS)

An environmental metric reflecting whether the exploitation of the vulnerability affects only the vulnerable component or has a broader impact within the organisation.

• Modified User Interaction (MUI)

An environmental metric indicates whether user interaction is required in the specific context of the organisation or environment.

• Prioritization

The process of ranking vulnerabilities based on their severity, impact, and exploitability to determine the order in which they should be addressed.

4.8 Summary

1. Vulnerability Discovery: Techniques and Tools

Vulnerability discovery involves identifying weaknesses in systems through various techniques and tools. Techniques include automated scanning, manual testing, and threat intelligence. Tools such as vulnerability scanners and penetration testing frameworks detect and report vulnerabilities. Effective discovery is essential for maintaining an up-to-date understanding of potential security issues.

2. Vulnerability Regression Testing

Vulnerability regression testing ensures that previously fixed vulnerabilities do not reappear after system updates or changes. This process involves re-testing the system to confirm that the applied fixes remain effective and that no new vulnerabilities have been introduced. Regression testing is crucial for maintaining long-term security and stability.

3. Responsible Disclosure Programs

Responsible disclosure programs provide a structured approach for security researchers and ethical hackers to report vulnerabilities to organisations. These programs ensure that vulnerabilities are disclosed in a manner that allows organisations to address the issues before they are publicly known, reducing the risk of exploitation. Effective programs include clear guidelines for reporting, communication, and remediation.

4. Vulnerability Analysis and Ranking

Vulnerability analysis and ranking involve evaluating identified vulnerabilities' severity and potential impact. This process uses metrics such as CVSS to assign severity scores, helping organisations prioritise vulnerabilities based on their risk to the organisation. Key components include threat intelligence, exploitability assessment, and business impact analysis. Advanced methods enhance these evaluations with contextual and dynamic considerations.

5. Common Vulnerability Scoring System (CVSS)

CVSS provides a standardised method for scoring the severity of vulnerabilities. It includes base metrics (e.g., attack vector, complexity), temporal metrics (e.g., exploit code maturity), and environmental metrics (e.g., business impact). CVSS scores help organisations prioritize vulnerabilities based on severity and potential impact, facilitating more informed risk management.

6. Advanced Vulnerability Scoring

Advanced vulnerability scoring extends beyond traditional metrics to offer more nuanced assessments. This includes integrating threat intelligence, analysing exploitability trends, and performing business impact analyses. Advanced methods provide a tailored approach to vulnerability prioritisation, considering dynamic threat landscapes and organisational contexts.

4.9 Previous Year Solved Questions

Question. How does a comprehensive vulnerability management program integrate techniques for vulnerability discovery, regression testing, responsible disclosure, and scoring, and what role does advanced vulnerability scoring play in enhancing the effectiveness of this program? (Delhi University, 2023 MCA)

Answer. A comprehensive vulnerability management program is a structured approach designed to identify, evaluate, prioritise, and address vulnerabilities within an organisation's systems and software. Integrating various techniques and practices into this program is crucial for maintaining a robust security posture. Here's how each component—vulnerability discovery, regression testing, responsible disclosure, and scoring—plays a role and the significance of advanced vulnerability scoring in enhancing the program's effectiveness:

1. Vulnerability Discovery

Vulnerability discovery is the first step in a vulnerability management program and involves identifying weaknesses in systems, applications, and networks. This process employs a range of techniques:

Automated Scanning: Tools such as vulnerability scanners automatically detect known vulnerabilities by analysing system configurations, code, and network traffic.

Manual Testing: Security professionals perform manual assessments, such as penetration testing, to find vulnerabilities that automated tools might miss.

Threat Intelligence: Integrating threat intelligence provides real-time Data on emerging threats and vulnerabilities, enhancing the discovery process by focusing efforts on the most relevant risks.

By combining these techniques, organisations can comprehensively identify vulnerabilities, setting the stage for effective management and remediation.

2. Vulnerability Regression Testing

Once vulnerabilities are discovered and addressed, regression testing ensures that the fixes remain effective over time. This process involves:

Re-Testing: Conducting tests to confirm that previously identified vulnerabilities have been resolved and that no new issues have been introduced.

Continuous Monitoring: Regularly updating tests to reflect changes in the system and new threat information.

Regression testing is crucial for verifying that remediation efforts are successful and that vulnerabilities do not resurface, thereby maintaining the system's security integrity.

3. Responsible Disclosure Programs

Responsible disclosure programs provide a framework for security researchers and ethical hackers to report vulnerabilities to organisations in a controlled and constructive manner. Key aspects include:

Reporting Guidelines: Clear protocols for reporting vulnerabilities, including contact methods and required information.

Communication Channels: Secure and confidential channels for communication between the reporter and the organisation.

Remediation and Coordination: Processes for addressing reported vulnerabilities and coordinating with the reporter to ensure timely fixes.

These programs help prevent the public disclosure of vulnerabilities before they are resolved, reducing the risk of exploitation and fostering collaboration between organisations and the security community.

4. Vulnerability Analysis and Ranking

Once vulnerabilities are discovered, they must be analysed and ranked to prioritise remediation efforts. This involves:

Severity Scoring: This involves using metrics such as those from the Common Vulnerability Scoring System (CVSS) to assign a severity score based on factors like attack vector, impact, and exploitability.

Business Impact Analysis: Evaluating the potential impact of vulnerabilities on business operations, including financial, operational, and reputational effects.

Risk Prioritization: Ranking vulnerabilities based on their severity and impact to focus on the most critical issues first.

Effective analysis and ranking ensure that resources are allocated to address the most significant vulnerabilities, improving overall security posture.

5. Advanced Vulnerability Scoring

Advanced vulnerability scoring builds on traditional scoring methods to provide a more nuanced and contextual evaluation of vulnerabilities. It incorporates:

Threat Intelligence Integration: Enriching vulnerability scores with real-time Data on active threats and exploit trends, enhancing the relevance and accuracy of the scoring.

Exploitability Trends: Assessing the likelihood of exploitation based on exploit code availability and usage trends.

Business Impact Considerations: Incorporating specific business context to understand how vulnerabilities might affect critical assets and operations.

Dynamic Adjustments: Continuously updating scores based on new information and changing conditions.

Advanced scoring enhances the vulnerability management program by providing a more detailed and context-specific assessment, allowing organizations to prioritise vulnerabilities based on the most current and relevant Data.

Exercises

Exercise 1 – Multiple Choice Questions

1. What does the Common Vulnerability Scoring System (CVSS) provide?

a) A framework for software development

b) A standardized framework for assessing vulnerability severity

c) A method for Data encryption
d) A tool for network monitoring

2. Which CVSS metric describes the complexity of an attack required to exploit a vulnerability?
a) Confidentiality Impact
b) Attack Vector
c) Attack Complexity
d) Exploit Code Maturity

Exercise 2 – True/False

1. The Modified Attack Vector (MAV) is an environmental metric reflecting the attack vector in the specific context of an organization.
2. Vulnerability Management includes processes such as identifying, evaluating, prioritizing, and addressing vulnerabilities.

Exercise 3 – Fill in the blanks

1. __________ is a CVSS metric indicating how the vulnerability is exploited, such as network, adjacent network, local, or physical.
2. __________ refers to the process of evaluating and understanding the nature, impact, and exploitability of identified vulnerabilities.

Exercise 4- Fill in the blanks with two options

1. The CVSS metric __________ measures the impact on the confidentiality of the affected system or Data, with options for none, low, or high.
2. __________ is a CVSS metric that indicates the availability and maturity of exploit code for a vulnerability.

Exercise 5- Rearrange the sentence

1. [Scoring / Vulnerability / Vulnerability Management / Framework / Scoring / Assessment / Comprehensive / Process]
2. [Prioritization / Vulnerabilities / Order / Determine / Addressed / Should / The / Which / They]

Exercise 6- Choose the Odd One Out

1. Attack Vector, Exploit Code Maturity, Confidentiality Impact, Scope
2. Dynamic Scoring Adjustments, Severity Scoring, Business Impact Analysis, Vulnerability Discovery

Exercise 7- Jumble words

1. SROIACNFOET
2. TNIMIIZRPAOIT

Exercise 8- Match case

1. Attack Vector
2. Exploitability Assessment
3. Integrity Impact
4. Threat Intelligence Integration

a) Measurement of impact on system integrity
b) Analysis of how easily a vulnerability can be exploited
c) How the vulnerability is exploited
d) Incorporation of threat Data for prioritization

Exercise 9- Assertion – Reason

1. Assertion: CVSS provides a standardized framework for scoring vulnerabilities.
Reason: CVSS metrics include Attack Vector, Attack Complexity, and Confidentiality Impact.
a) Both Assertion and Reason are correct and Reason is the correct explanation for Assertion.

b) Both Assertion and Reason are correct but Reason is not the correct explanation for Assertion.
c) Assertion is correct but Reason is incorrect.
d) Assertion is incorrect but Reason is correct.

2. Assertion: Business Impact Analysis is not a part of vulnerability management.
Reason: Business Impact Analysis assesses the consequences of vulnerabilities on business operations.
a) Both Assertion and Reason are correct and Reason is the correct explanation for Assertion.
b) Both Assertion and Reason are correct but Reason is not the correct explanation for Assertion.
c) Assertion is correct but Reason is incorrect.
d) Assertion is incorrect but Reason is correct.

Exercise 10- Read the questions given below and find the appropriate word in the grid provided.
Questions:

1. The process of identifying weaknesses in systems through techniques such as automated scanning and tools like vulnerability scanners is known as __________.
2. The technique that ensures previously fixed vulnerabilities do not reappear after system updates or changes is called __________.

Grid:

M	H	O	A	I	J	B	J	Q	N	L	H	W	A	V	E	C
V	U	L	N	E	R	A	B	I	L	I	T	B	D	O	T	Y
M	K	E	P	O	P	V	N	M	P	Y	H	E	S	D	H	E
D	A	I	S	N	E	S	S	N	O	U	R	E	D	E	I	R
A	R	P	S	P	O	O	F	I	N	K	W	R	T	B	C	G
T	M	N	O	S	A	F	L	H	K	L	V	A	G	A	S	A
T	Q	W	O	T	R	C	A	G	W	M	G	E	F	R	I	L
R	E	G	R	E	S	S	I	O	N	T	E	S	T	I	N	G

Exercise 11- One- word

1. What is the term for a weakness or flaw in a system that can be exploited by attackers?
2. What is the term for the process of evaluating the characteristics and potential impact of identified vulnerabilities?

Exercise 12- Small Answers

1. Define Attack Vector.
2. What is Exploit Code Maturity?

Exercise 13- Long Answers

1. Explain the concept of Threat Intelligence Integration in vulnerability management.
2. Describe the importance of Vulnerability Regression Testing.

Exercise 14- Previous Year Unsolved Questions

1. Critically examine the copyright issues in digital medium. (IGNOU, December 2023, MCA)
2. Discuss the law in United States for regulation of cyberspace. (IGNOU, December 2023, MCA)
3. What is meant by Cryptography? Discuss RSA algorithm. (IGNOU, December 2023, MCA)
4. (a) What is cyber forensics? Explain with the help of an example.
   (b) What is Trademark? What are the different types of remedies available against infringement of trademark? (IGNOU, June 2023, MCA)
5. (a) What is a transposition cipher? Explain with the help of an example.

(b) What is confidentiality and availability of Data in the context of Data security? Explain how confidentiality can be maintained and availability can be ensured in a Data management system.

(c) What are the liabilities of network service providers in the context of cyber crimes? Explain.

(d) What are the possible trademark infringements related to search engines? Explain.

6. Describe the following issues related to cyberspace:
    a) Distributed denial of service attack
    b) Malwares
    c) Crypto jacking
    d) Cyber physical attack
    e) Phishing (IGNOU, December 2023, MCA)
7. (a) What are the advantages and disadvantages of symmetric-key cryptography?
    (b) Explain the following security measures:
    a) E-mail security
    b) Anti-virus protection
    c) Access security (IGNOU, December 2023, MCA)
8. Explain the term evidence and different types of evidence. (Mumbai University, December 2023, MCA)
9. Write Key IT requirements for SOX and HIPAA. (Mumbai University, December 2023, MCA)

Answers

Exercise 1- 1. **b)** A standardized framework for assessing vulnerability severity, 2. **c)** Attack Complexity
Exercise 2- 1. Attack Vector, 2. Vulnerability Analysis
Exercise 3- 1. True, 2. True
Exercise 4- 1. (Dynamic Scoring Adjustments / Exploitability Trends), 2. (Business Impact Analysis / Severity Scoring)
Exercise 5- 1. The Common Vulnerability Scoring System (CVSS) is used to assess the severity of vulnerabilities.
Exercise 6- 1. Modified Attack Vector (The others are basic CVSS metrics, while MAV is environmental), 2. Report Confidence (The others are metrics related to exploitability).
Exercise 7- 1. Wulrenbiatly – Vulnerability, 2. Msocosroing – Scoring System
Exercise 8- 1– d) , 2 – a), 3 – b) , 4 – c)
Exercise 9- Assertion (A): Dynamic Scoring Adjustments improve vulnerability management. **Reason (R)**: They update vulnerability scores based on real-time threat intelligence.
Answer: Both A and R are correct, and R explains A.
Exercise10 – 1. Vulnerability , 2. Regression Testing

M	H	O	A	I	J	B	J	Q	N	L	H	W	A	V	E	C
V	U	L	N	E	R	A	B	I	L	I	T	B	D	O	T	Y
M	K	E	P	O	P	V	N	M	P	Y	H	E	S	D	H	E
D	A	I	S	N	E	S	S	N	O	U	R	E	D	E	I	R
A	R	P	S	P	O	O	F	I	N	K	W	R	T	B	C	G
T	M	N	O	S	A	F	L	H	K	L	V	A	G	A	S	A
T	Q	W	O	T	R	C	A	G	W	M	G	E	F	R	I	L
R	E	G	R	E	S	S	I	O	N	T	E	S	T	I	N	G

Exercise 11- 1. Attack Vector, 2. Threat Intelligence

Test Paper

Chapter-4

Vulnerability Management

Time Duration: 30 Minutes **Maximum Marks: 25**

General Instructions:

1. The question paper consists of 12 questions and is divided into four sections, A, B, C and D.
2. All questions are compulsory.
3. Section A comprises MCQs, Fill in the blanks and True or False carrying one marks each.
4. Section B comprises VSAQs(very short answers questions) carrying two marks each.
5. Section C comprises SAQs(short questions) carrying four marks each.
6. Section D comprises long questions carrying five marks each.

SECTION-A

I. Multiple choice questions: **(1*2=2)**

1. What does the Common Vulnerability Scoring System (CVSS) provide?

a) A framework for software development
b) A standardized framework for assessing vulnerability severity
c) A method for Data encryption
d) A tool for network monitoring

2. Which CVSS metric describes the complexity of an attack required to exploit a vulnerability?

a) Confidentiality Impact
b) Attack Vector
c) Attack Complexity
d) Exploit Code Maturity

II. Fill in the blanks: **(1*2=2)**

1. __________ is a CVSS metric indicating how the vulnerability is exploited, such as network, adjacent network, local, or physical.

2. __________ refers to the process of evaluating and understanding the nature, impact, and exploitability of identified vulnerabilities.

III. True or False: **(1*2=2)**

1. The Modified Attack Vector (MAV) is an environmental metric reflecting the attack vector in the specific context of an organization.

2. Vulnerability Management includes processes such as identifying, evaluating, prioritizing, and addressing vulnerabilities.

SECTION-B

IV. Very Short answers type questions-I **(2*3=6)**

1. Define Attack Vector.
2. What is Exploit Code Maturity?
3. Explain the term "Vulnerability Management".

SECTION-C

V. Short answers type questions-II **(4*2=8)**

1. Describe how Dynamic Scoring Adjustments affect vulnerability management.

2. What are the key components of the Common Vulnerability Scoring System (CVSS) and their significance?

SECTION-D

VI. Long answers type questions **(5*1=5)**

1. Discuss the role of Threat Intelligence Integration in improving vulnerability management.

ONLINE RESOURCES

Practice Paper

Link: https://forms.gle/qtw9JvqZDYdGGmeZ9

QR Code:

YouTube Video Playlist Link

Link: https://www.youtube.com/playlist?list=PLzlh_31VWEFpGMEC_dHVJPS7agg6h8cu5

QR Code:

Chapter 5 - Web Penetration Testing

In this chapter, you will learn about:

Web Intrusion/Penetration Test Workflow
OWASP Checklist for Web Intrusion Tests
Identifying Hidden Web Contents
Testing for Personal Information Exposure Vulnerabilities
Web Application API Testing
Testing Authentication Mechanisms
Session Management Weaknesses
Testing Authorization Layers
Exploiting Web Application
Reporting and Documenting Penetration Test Findings

Web penetration testing, often referred to as ethical hacking or security testing, is a critical practice for identifying and addressing security vulnerabilities in web applications. As web applications become increasingly integral to business operations and online interactions, ensuring their security is paramount to protecting sensitive Data, maintaining user trust, and safeguarding against potential cyber threats. Web penetration testing is a simulated cyberattack on a web application, designed to uncover security weaknesses that could be exploited by malicious actors. The goal is to assess the application's security posture by identifying vulnerabilities, misconfigurations, and potential exploit paths before they can be used in real-world attacks.

5.1 Web Intrusion/Penetration Test Workflow

The workflow for web intrusion or penetration testing is a systematic approach designed to assess the security of web applications. It involves a series of structured phases, each aimed at uncovering vulnerabilities, evaluating their impact, and providing recommendations for remediation. Below is a detailed breakdown of the key stages in a typical web penetration test workflow:

1. Planning and Preparation

Objective: Define the scope, objectives, and methodology of the penetration test.

Define Scope: Identify the web application(s) to be tested, including their components, interfaces, and boundaries. Specify any excluded areas or systems to avoid unintended disruptions.

Establish Goals: Set clear objectives for the test, such as identifying specific vulnerabilities, assessing security controls, or simulating particular attack scenarios.

Agree on Rules of Engagement: Outline the testing parameters, including testing methods, allowed tools, and reporting protocols. Establish communication channels and protocols for incident response.

Obtain Authorization: Secure explicit permission from stakeholders or owners of the web application to conduct the test, ensuring legal and organizational compliance.

2. Reconnaissance

Objective: Gather information about the web application to identify potential attack vectors.

Passive Reconnaissance: Collect information without directly interacting with the target, such as through public sources, domain registries, and social engineering. This includes identifying technologies used, third-party services, and potential entry points.

Active Reconnaissance: Engage with the web application to gather detailed information, such as performing DNS lookups, network scans, and banner grabbing. This phase helps build a comprehensive profile of the target.

3. Scanning and Enumeration

Objective: Identify and catalogue potential vulnerabilities and weaknesses within the web application.

Port Scanning: Detect open ports and services running on the web server to understand the attack surface.

Vulnerability Scanning: Use automated tools to scan for known vulnerabilities, misconfigurations, and security weaknesses. This may include scanning for outdated software versions, missing patches, and insecure configurations.

Enumeration: Gather detailed information about the web application's components, such as directories, files, and user accounts. This helps in identifying potential targets for exploitation.

4. Exploitation

Objective: Attempt to exploit identified vulnerabilities to determine their impact and verify their existence.

Vulnerability Exploitation: Use manual techniques or automated tools to exploit vulnerabilities and gain unauthorized access or control over the web application. This may involve SQL injection, cross-site scripting (XSS), or other attack methods.
Privilege Escalation: Attempt to escalate privileges or gain higher levels of access within the application to assess the extent of potential damage.
Session Management: Test session management mechanisms, such as authentication and authorization controls, to identify weaknesses in session handling and access controls.

5. Post-Exploitation

Objective: Assess the impact of successful exploitation and gather additional information if necessary.
Data Extraction: Collect and analyze Data obtained through exploitation to evaluate the impact on the web application and its users.
Persistence: Determine whether it is possible to maintain access or establish a persistent foothold within the application for future exploitation.

6. Reporting

Objective: Document findings, provide a detailed analysis, and recommend remediation steps.
Findings Documentation: Prepare a comprehensive report detailing identified vulnerabilities, their impact, and the methods used to discover and exploit them. Include evidence such as screenshots, logs, and descriptions of the vulnerabilities.
Risk Assessment: Evaluate the severity of each vulnerability and its potential impact on the web application and organization. Provide a risk rating to prioritize remediation efforts.
Remediation Recommendations: Offer actionable recommendations for addressing identified vulnerabilities, including specific changes to configuration, code, or security controls.
Executive Summary: Provide a high-level overview of the findings and recommendations for stakeholders who may not require detailed technical information.

7. Remediation and Follow-Up

Objective: Address identified vulnerabilities and verify the effectiveness of remediation efforts.
Remediation Implementation: Work with the development and operations teams to implement recommended fixes and security improvements.
Re-Testing: Perform follow-up testing to ensure that vulnerabilities have been successfully addressed and that no new issues have been introduced.
Continuous Improvement: Use insights from the test to enhance overall security practices, update policies, and improve security posture.

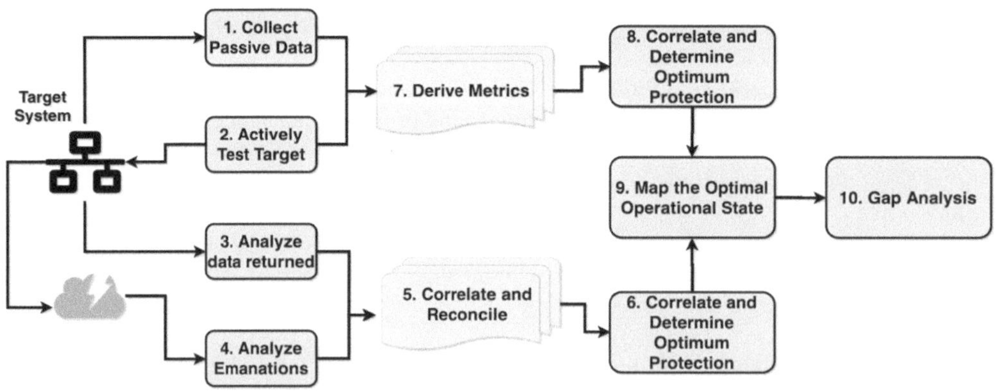

5.2 OWASP Checklist for Web Intrusion Tests

The OWASP (Open Web Application Security Project) checklist for web intrusion tests is a comprehensive set of guidelines and best practices to ensure that all potential security vulnerabilities are considered during a web penetration test. The checklist covers critical areas of web application security, focusing on identifying common vulnerabilities, misconfigurations, and weaknesses.
The following is a summary of key points typically found in the OWASP checklist for conducting a web intrusion test:

1. Input Validation

- **Injection Attacks**: Test for SQL Injection (SQLi), OS Command Injection, and LDAP Injection vulnerabilities.
- **Cross-Site Scripting (XSS)**: Check for reflected, stored, and DOM-based XSS vulnerabilities.
- **File Uploads**: Verify that file uploads are properly sanitized and that dangerous file types (e.g., executable scripts) are restricted.
- **Buffer Overflow**: Check for buffer overflow vulnerabilities, especially in input fields where large Data inputs may occur.

2. Authentication and Session Management

- **Broken Authentication**: Ensure that authentication mechanisms are robust and resistant to brute-force, dictionary, and credential stuffing attacks.
- **Session Fixation**: Test for vulnerabilities where a user's session ID can be fixed or predicted.
- **Session Timeout**: Verify proper session expiration and idle timeout policies are in place.
- **Password Policies**: Ensure the application enforces strong password policies, such as complexity requirements, length, and regular expiration.

3. Access Control and Authorization

- **Privilege Escalation**: Test for vertical and horizontal privilege escalation vulnerabilities.
- **Insecure Direct Object References (IDOR)**: Ensure users cannot access unauthorized resources by manipulating object identifiers (e.g., URL paths, parameters).
- **Role-Based Access Control (RBAC)**: Confirm that different roles (e.g., admin, user) are properly enforced and cannot be bypassed.
- **Forced Browsing**: Test for unauthorized access to restricted files, directories, or administrative interfaces by directly accessing URLs.

4. Sensitive Data Exposure

- **Data Encryption**: Check that sensitive Data (e.g., passwords, payment details) is encrypted both in transit (via TLS/SSL) and at rest.
- **Sensitive Information Disclosure**: Ensure that sensitive Data is not inadvertently exposed in error messages, logs, or URLs.
- **Weak Cryptography**: Verify that strong cryptographic algorithms are used for encryption and hashing, avoiding outdated algorithms like MD5 or SHA-1.

5. Cross-Site Request Forgery (CSRF)

- **CSRF Protection**: Ensure that the application implements anti-CSRF tokens and that these tokens are unique and tied to the user's session.
- **State-Changing Requests**: Verify that critical actions (e.g., password changes, financial transactions) are protected against CSRF attacks.

6. Security Misconfiguration

- **Default Credentials**: Ensure that default passwords and usernames are changed for all services and components.
- **Error Handling**: Check that error messages do not reveal sensitive information about the underlying infrastructure.
- **Secure Headers**: Validate the use of security-related HTTP headers such as Content-Security-Policy (CSP), Strict-Transport-Security (HSTS), and X-Frame-Options.

7. Insecure Deserialization

- **Deserialization Vulnerabilities**: Test for deserialization flaws where untrusted Data could lead to remote code execution, privilege escalation, or other harmful actions.
- **Input Validation for Serialized Data**: Ensure proper validation of serialized and deserialized Data to prevent tampering.

8. Cross-Origin Resource Sharing (CORS)

- **Misconfigured CORS**: Ensure that the application does not allow cross-origin requests from unauthorized or dangerous domains.
- **Access Control Policies**: Verify that CORS policies are correctly configured to restrict the domains allowed to access resources.

9. Security Logging and Monitoring

- **Audit Trails**: Ensure that the application logs important security events (e.g., login attempts, changes to sensitive Data).
- **Log Tampering**: Check that logs are secure and cannot be easily modified or deleted by attackers.
- **Intrusion Detection**: Verify that mechanisms for detecting and responding to potential intrusion attempts (e.g., alerting, logging) are in place.

10. Web and API Security

• **API Security**: Test for security weaknesses in APIs exposed by the web application, including authentication, rate limiting, and input validation.

• **Security of External Integrations**: Verify the security of third-party integrations such as payment gateways, OAuth, and other external services.

11. Business Logic Vulnerabilities

• **Business Logic Testing**: Identify potential flaws in the application's logic that could allow users to bypass intended workflows or gain unauthorized access to resources.

• **Transaction Manipulation**: Ensure that critical transactions (e.g., financial transactions) cannot be manipulated or bypassed through vulnerabilities like race conditions or improper validation.

12. Use of Components with Known Vulnerabilities

• **Outdated Libraries and Frameworks**: Check that all third-party components (e.g., libraries, frameworks) are up to date and free of known security vulnerabilities.

• **Dependency Management**: Ensure that the application has proper processes in place for managing and updating dependencies.

13. Denial of Service (DoS)

• **Rate Limiting**: Test for the presence of rate-limiting mechanisms that prevent brute-force attacks and service overloads.

• **Resource Exhaustion:** Verify that the application can handle large-scale input and traffic without becoming unresponsive or crashing.

5.3 Identifying Hidden Web Contents

Identifying hidden web content involves discovering files, directories, or resources that are not immediately visible or linked within a web application but may still be accessible and pose security risks. These hidden elements often include sensitive information, configuration files, or backup copies that attackers can exploit.

Key Techniques for Identifying Hidden Content:

1. Directory Brute-Forcing: Using automated tools (e.g., DirBuster, Gobuster) to systematically guess common directory and file names.
2. Spidering: Crawling the web application to discover unlinked content.
3. Predictable File/Directory Names: Searching for predictable filenames (e.g., admin, backup, config).
4. Backup Files: Identifying backup files (e.g., .bak, .old, .zip) left on the server.
5. Misconfigured Permissions: Exploiting directory listing if improperly configured.
6. Parameter Fuzzing: Manipulating parameters in URLs or forms to access hidden resources.

Conclusion:

Identifying hidden web contents is a crucial step in penetration testing to prevent attackers from accessing sensitive files or directories that could be exploited for further attacks. Regular audits and automated tools help secure web applications from such risks.

5.4 Testing for Personal Information Exposure

Testing for personal information exposure involves identifying vulnerabilities where sensitive user Data (e.g., names, addresses, passwords, credit card numbers) is unintentionally exposed. This can lead to privacy violations, identity theft, and regulatory non-compliance (e.g., GDPR, CCPA).

Key Steps in Testing:

1. Inspect Input/Output Data:

Examine forms and API responses to ensure personal Data is handled securely.

Test for exposure in GET parameters, cookies, and headers.

2. Check for Data Leaks:

Analyze error messages, logs, and debug information for sensitive Data exposure.

Ensure proper sanitization of log files and error reporting.

3. Unencrypted Data:

Verify that sensitive Data is transmitted securely using HTTPS and encrypted storage methods (e.g., passwords hashed with strong algorithms).

4. API Testing:

Test API endpoints for overexposed personal Data in responses, especially during resource fetching.

Ensure proper access control is enforced.

5. Session Management:
Test for weaknesses in session handling that may expose user Data in URL, cookies, or session tokens.

5.5 Web Application API Testing

API testing in web applications involves evaluating the APIs' security, functionality, and performance that facilitate communication between different software components. Since APIs often handle sensitive Data and critical business logic, they are a prime target for attackers.

Key Aspects of Web Application API Testing:

1. Authentication and Authorization:
Ensure APIs use strong authentication mechanisms (e.g., OAuth, JWT) and proper role-based access controls.
Test for vulnerabilities like broken authentication, where users may gain unauthorised access.

2. Input Validation:
Check for injection vulnerabilities (e.g., SQL, XML, JSON injections).
Ensure all inputs are validated and sanitised before being processed by the API.

3. Rate Limiting:
Test APIs for rate-limiting mechanisms to prevent abuse, such as brute-force or denial-of-service (DoS) attacks.

4. Error Handling:
Verify that error messages do not expose sensitive information, such as stack traces or internal details of the API.

5. Data Exposure:
Ensure that sensitive Data (e.g., passwords, tokens, personal information) is not exposed in API responses.
Test for overexposure in API responses, especially with bulk Data queries or resource fetching.

6. Session Management:
Test for proper session handling and secure token storage.
Ensure that tokens expire after a reasonable time and cannot be reused.

5.6 Testing Authentication Mechanisms

Testing authentication mechanisms is essential to ensure a web application effectively protects against unauthorised access and account compromise. Authentication mechanisms include login processes, password management, multi-factor authentication (MFA), and session handling. Testing aims to identify vulnerabilities that could allow attackers to bypass authentication controls.

Key Areas for Testing Authentication:

1. Brute Force and Dictionary Attacks:
- o Test for rate-limiting on login attempts to prevent attackers from guessing passwords.
- o Ensure CAPTCHA or other mechanisms are in place to defend against automated login attempts.

2. Weak Password Policies:
- o Evaluate password complexity requirements (length, special characters, etc.).
- o Ensure proper enforcement of password rules, such as preventing the use of common or easily guessable passwords.

3. Password Reset and Recovery:
- o Test password reset mechanisms to ensure they are secure (e.g., via email verification or security questions).
- o Ensure recovery links and tokens expire after a reasonable time and are single-use.

4. Multi-Factor Authentication (MFA):
- o Verify that MFA is implemented and required for sensitive actions.
- o Ensure that second-factor codes (e.g., OTP, push notifications) are delivered securely.

5. Session Management:
- o Test for secure session token generation, ensuring that tokens are random and difficult to guess.
- o Verify that session expiration and logout functionalities work as expected.
- o Test for session fixation vulnerabilities, where attackers may hijack a user's session by setting their session ID.

6. Default or Weak Credentials:
- o Ensure default credentials for admin panels or third-party components are removed or changed.
- o Test for the presence of weak default passwords.

7. Secure Storage of Credentials:
- o Verify that passwords are stored securely using hashing solid algorithms (e.g., bcrypt, PBKDF2).

o Ensure that sensitive Data is never stored in plaintext, Databases, or logs.

8. Authorization and Access Control:

o Test the authorisation process to ensure that authenticated users only access resources or features appropriate to their roles.

5.7 Glossary

• **Penetration Testing:** A simulated attack on a system, network, or application to identify vulnerabilities that attackers could exploit. It involves actively probing for weaknesses to assess security posture.

• **OWASP Checklist: A** comprehensive guide from the Open Web Application Security Project (OWASP) used during penetration tests to ensure all common vulnerabilities are covered and addressed.

• **Hidden Web Contents**: Files, directories, or information not directly visible to users but may be accessible through specific URLs, endpoints, or directory structures. These contents often contain sensitive information or functionality.

• **Personal Information Exposure**: When sensitive user Data (e.g., names, addresses, passwords) is unintentionally exposed to unauthorised users, often due to weak security controls or poor Data handling practices.

• **API Testing:** The process of testing application programming interfaces (APIs) to identify security flaws, ensure proper functionality, and verify that Data handling is secure and authorised users have appropriate access.

• **Authentication Mechanisms**: Processes used to verify the identity of users, typically involving credentials like usernames, passwords, and sometimes multi-factor authentication (MFA).

• **Session Management:** The system that tracks a user's interactions with a web application across multiple requests. Secure session management ensures that sessions are protected from hijacking or misuse.

• **Authorization Layers:** The set of controls that determine what a user can do once authenticated, ensuring that users can only access resources and perform actions they are authorised for.

• **Privilege Escalation:** A type of attack where a lower-privileged user gains access to higher-level privileges, often through exploiting vulnerabilities in authorisation mechanisms.

• **Insecure Direct Object References (IDOR):** A vulnerability that occurs when an application exposes references to internal objects (such as files or Database records) without proper access controls, allowing unauthorised users to access them by modifying parameters.

• **Cross-Site Scripting (XSS):** A vulnerability where attackers inject malicious scripts into web pages, which are then executed in the browser of other users. This can lead to Data theft, session hijacking, or defacement.

• **SQL Injection (SQLi):** A code injection technique where an attacker exploits vulnerabilities in a web application's Database query handling by inserting malicious SQL queries through user input fields.

• **Cross-Site Request Forgery (CSRF):** An attack where a malicious website tricks a user's browser into sending unauthorised requests to a different site where the user is authenticated, potentially leading to unauthorised actions.

• **Security Misconfigurations**: Weaknesses introduced by improper configuration of software, hardware, or network components, often exposing unnecessary services, credentials, or detailed error messages.

• **Exploitation:** Taking advantage of identified vulnerabilities to gain unauthorised access, control, or Data from a target system or application.

• **Proof of Concept (PoC):** Demonstrations used in penetration testing to show how vulnerabilities can be exploited, often including evidence such as payloads, screenshots, or logs.

• Risk Ranking is the process of assigning a severity level to identified vulnerabilities based on factors like ease of exploitation, potential impact, and likelihood of attack.

• **Remediation Plan:** A set of recommended actions to fix vulnerabilities, mitigate risks, and improve the security of an application or system.

5.8 Summary

• **Web Intrusion/Penetration Test Workflow:** This section outlines the systematic approach to penetration testing, including phases such as reconnaissance, scanning, exploitation, and reporting. It emphasises the importance of following a structured workflow to ensure thorough and effective testing.

• **OWASP Checklist for Web Intrusion Tests:** The OWASP Checklist provides a comprehensive guide for penetration testers to evaluate web applications against common security risks. It ensures that critical vulnerabilities, as identified by OWASP, are systematically addressed during testing.

• **Identifying Hidden Web Contents:** This section focuses on discovering files, directories, and resources that are not directly visible or linked within a web application. Identifying hidden contents is crucial as they may contain sensitive information or pose security risks if accessed by unauthorised users.

• **Testing for Personal Information Exposure:** It highlights the importance of protecting sensitive personal Data and not unintentionally exposing it. Testing involves checking for vulnerabilities that could lead to Data leaks and ensuring compliance with Data protection regulations.
• **Web Application API Testing:** This section discusses the testing of application programming interfaces (APIs) to identify security flaws, ensure proper functionality, and validate that APIs handle Data securely. API testing is crucial for maintaining the integrity and security of communication between software components.
• **Testing Authentication Mechanisms:** It covers evaluating authentication processes, including password policies, multi-factor authentication (MFA), and session handling. Proper testing ensures that authentication mechanisms are robust and protect against unauthorised access.
• **Session Management Weaknesses:** This section addresses common session management issues, such as hijacking, fixation, and insecure session storage. Effective session management prevents unauthorised access and maintains user session security.
• **Testing Authorization Layers:** It focuses on verifying that users can only access resources and perform their authorised actions. It includes testing for privilege escalation, access control, and insecure direct object references (IDOR) to ensure proper authorisation mechanisms are in place.
• **Exploiting Web Application Vulnerabilities:** This paper discusses the process of leveraging identified vulnerabilities to understand their potential impact. It covers common vulnerabilities like SQL injection, XSS, and CSRF and highlights techniques for exploiting these weaknesses to demonstrate their risks.
• **Reporting and Documenting Penetration Test Findings:** This final section emphasises the importance of clear and comprehensive reporting. It includes summarising findings, risk ranking, providing remediation recommendations, and documenting the testing process to ensure effective communication and follow-up actions.

5.9 Previous Year Solved Questions

Question. How does the process of web penetration testing ensure the security of web applications, and what are the critical steps involved in conducting a practical penetration test? (Delhi University, 2021 MCA)
Answer. Web penetration testing is a crucial process for ensuring the security of web applications by systematically identifying and addressing vulnerabilities that attackers could exploit. This process involves well-defined steps, each evaluating different aspects of an application's security posture. Here's a comprehensive overview of how web penetration testing ensures security and the key steps involved:

1. Planning and Scoping

Planning and scoping is the initial phase where the penetration test's objectives, scope, and limitations are defined. This involves:
1. **Defining Objectives**: Establishing the test's goals, such as identifying critical vulnerabilities or assessing compliance with security standards.
2. **Scope Definition**: Determining which systems, applications, or components will be tested. This includes identifying the boundaries to ensure the test does not impact production environments or violate legal constraints.
3. **Resource Allocation**: This includes assigning the appropriate tools and resources needed for the test, selecting the testing team, and gathering necessary permissions.

2. Reconnaissance

During **reconnaissance**, information about the target application is collected to understand its structure and potential entry points. This phase includes:
1. **Passive Reconnaissance**: Gathering information without directly interacting with the target, such as through public records, social media, or DNS queries.
2. **Active Reconnaissance**: Directly engaging with the target to obtain detailed information, such as performing network scans, discovering open ports, and identifying services running on the application.

3. Scanning and Enumeration

Scanning and enumeration involve actively probing the application to identify vulnerabilities and gather detailed information:
1. **Vulnerability Scanning**: Using automated tools to detect common vulnerabilities such as SQL injection, XSS, and security misconfigurations. Tools like OWASP ZAP or Nessus may be employed.
2. **Port Scanning**: Identifying open ports and services running on the application to assess potential entry points.
3. **Enumeration**: Gathering detailed information about the application's components, user accounts, and network structure.

4. Exploitation

In the **exploitation** phase, testers exploit identified vulnerabilities to determine their impact. This involves:

1. Proof of Concept (PoC): Demonstrating how vulnerabilities can be exploited to compromise the application or access sensitive Data. This may include injecting malicious payloads or manipulating input fields.
2. Privilege Escalation: Attempting to gain higher privileges or access restricted application areas, such as admin panels or Sensitive Data.
3. Session Management: Testing for weaknesses in session handling, such as session fixation or hijacking, to assess the security of user sessions.

5. Post-Exploitation and Reporting

Post-exploitation involves assessing the extent of the compromise and determining the potential impact of the vulnerabilities:

1. Data Extraction: Analyzing the Data accessed during exploitation to understand the extent of the breach and identify sensitive information that could be at risk.
2. Cleanup: Ensure that any changes made during testing are reversed and that no residual vulnerabilities remain in the system.
3. Reporting: Documenting the findings in a comprehensive report, including:
a. Executive Summary: A high-level overview of the test results and overall security posture tailored for non-technical stakeholders.
b. Vulnerability Details: Detailed descriptions of identified vulnerabilities, including proof of concept, risk assessment, and impact analysis.
c. Recommendations: Actionable steps for remediation, prioritising based on the severity of the findings.
d. Technical Appendices: Supporting documentation such as logs, screenshots, and detailed technical analysis for developers and security teams.

6. Remediation and Follow-Up

The final phase involves **remediation** and **follow-up** to address the vulnerabilities identified during the test:
1. Remediation: Implementing the recommended fixes and improvements to address the vulnerabilities. This may involve code changes, configuration updates, or patching vulnerabilities.
2. Retesting: Conducting follow-up tests to verify that the vulnerabilities have been successfully addressed and that no new issues have been introduced.

Exercises

Exercise 1 – Multiple Choice Questions

1. What is the primary goal of penetration testing?
a) Prevent all attacks
b) Simulate attacks to identify vulnerabilities
c) Block unauthorized users
d) Enhance user experience

2. What vulnerability allows an attacker to access hidden files and directories in a web application?
a) SQL Injection
b) Hidden Web Contents
c) Cross-Site Scripting (XSS)
d) Authentication Mechanisms

Exercise 2 – True/False

1. Cross-Site Scripting (XSS) vulnerabilities allow attackers to inject scripts that execute in the victim's browser.
2. API Testing is used to identify hidden web contents.

Exercise 3 – Fill in the blanks

1. __________ is an attack where a lower-privileged user gains unauthorized higher-level access.
2. When testing web applications, ___________ ensures proper Data handling between components.

Exercise 4- Fill in the blanks with two options

1. ___________ (Session Hijacking/Session Management) is an attack where a malicious actor takes control of an active user session.

2. ___________ (SQL Injection/IDOR) allows attackers to directly access internal objects by manipulating URL parameters.

Exercise 5- Rearrange the sentence

1. conducted tests / to verify / are performed / Penetration testing / vulnerabilities and security flaws.
2. sensitive / Hidden web contents / contain / files or directories / information / that is not

Exercise 6- Choose the Odd One Out

1. a) SQL Injection
b) XSS
c) Privilege Escalation
d) Password Hashing

2. a) CSRF
b) API Testing
c) Session Fixation
d) Insecure Direct Object Reference (IDOR)

Exercise 7- Jumble words

1. SROSC-ITE XGINTRCPS (A common vulnerability involving malicious script injection in web browsers).
2. USEOSN HKGIAJNIC (A type of attack where an attacker takes over a valid user session).

Exercise 8- Match case

1. Cross-Site Scripting (XSS)
2. API Testing
3. Penetration Testing
4. Session Hijacking

A. Simulates an attack to identify weaknesses
B. Stealing or guessing session tokens
C. Testing security and functionality of APIs
D. Injecting malicious scripts into websites

Exercise 9- Assertion – Reason

1. Assertion: API testing is an important aspect of penetration testing.
Reason: APIs handle secure Data and validate user access rights.
a) Both Assertion and Reason are true, and Reason explains Assertion
b) Both Assertion and Reason are true, but Reason does not explain Assertion
c) Assertion is true, but Reason is false
d) Both Assertion and Reason are false

2. Assertion: Session management weaknesses can lead to unauthorized access.
Reason: Proper session handling prevents session hijacking.
a) Both Assertion and Reason are true, and Reason explains Assertion
b) Both Assertion and Reason are true, but Reason does not explain Assertion
c) Assertion is true, but Reason is false
d) Both Assertion and Reason are false

Exercise 10- Read the questions given below and find the appropriate word in the grid provided.
Questions:

1. The systematic approach to penetration testing that includes phases such as reconnaissance, scanning, exploitation, and reporting is known as __________.

2. The process of evaluating authentication processes, including password policies and multi-factor authentication (MFA), to ensure robustness and protection against unauthorized access is referred to as __________.

Grid:

P	E	N	E	T	R	A	T	I	O	N	T	E	S	T	E	W	C
V	U	L	N	E	R	A	B	I	L	I	T	B	D	O	T	E	Y
M	K	E	P	O	P	V	N	M	P	Y	H	E	S	D	H	R	E
D	A	I	S	N	E	S	S	N	O	U	R	E	D	E	I	A	R
A	R	P	S	P	O	O	F	I	N	K	W	R	T	B	C	C	G
T	E	S	T	A	U	T	H	E	N	T	I	C	A	T	I	O	N
T	Q	W	O	T	R	C	A	G	W	M	G	E	F	R	I	E	L
R	E	G	R	E	S	S	I	O	N	T	E	S	T	I	N	Q	G

Exercise 11- One- word

1. What is the process of simulating an attack to identify security vulnerabilities called?
2. Which vulnerability involves attackers gaining unauthorized access by manipulating URL parameters?

Exercise 12- Small Answers

1. Explain the importance of session management in web application security.
2. What is OWASP, and why is it significant in penetration testing?

Exercise 13- Long Answers

1. Describe the process of penetration testing, including the steps involved in identifying and exploiting vulnerabilities.
2. Explain SQL Injection and its impact on web application security.

Exercise 14- Previous Year Unsolved Questions

1. Explain the difference between Cross-Site Scripting (XSS) and Cross-Site Request Forgery (CSRF). (Mumbai University, 2022)
2. Discuss the importance of secure session handling in preventing session hijacking.). (Mumbai University, 2022)
3. What are the needs of regulating cyberspace? Explain. (IGNOU, December 2023, MCA)
4. Explain the role of filtering devices and rating systems in the context of legal and self-regulatory framework of cyberspace. (IGNOU, December 2023, MCA)
5. Explain the following terms in the context of cyber crimes, cyber laws, and IPR issues:
a) Cyber Forensics
b) Classification of cyber crimes
c) Domain name disputes
d) Framing (IGNOU, December 2023, MCA)
6. Attempt any four of the following
a) List general guidelines for password policies
b) Difference between virus and worm
c) How cybercrimes differs from most terrestrial crimes
d) What are different Security Risks for Organization
e) What are mobile vulnerabilities? (Mumbai University, January 2023, MCA)
7. Discuss steps involved in planning of cyber attacks by criminal. (Mumbai University, January 2023, MCA)

Answers

Exercise 1- 1. b) To simulate attacks and identify weaknesses, 2. c) OWASP Checklist
Exercise 2- 1. True, 2. False
Exercise 3- 1. Privilege Escalation, 2. API Testing
Exercise 4- 1. Session Hijacking, 2. IDOR (Insecure Direct Object References)
Exercise 5- 1. Penetration testing is performed to verify vulnerabilities and conduct security flaw tests., 2. Hidden web contents contain files or directories that are not directly visible and often contain sensitive information.
Exercise 6- 1. d) Password Hashing (Others are vulnerabilities, while password hashing is a security measure)2. API Testing (Others are vulnerabilities, API Testing is a process)
Exercise 7- 1. Cross-Site Scripting, 2. Session Hijacking
Exercise 8- 1-d, 2-c, 3-a, 4-c
Exercise 9- 1. a) Both Assertion and Reason are true, and Reason explains Assertion, 2. a) Both Assertion and Reason are true, and Reason explains Assertion
Exercise 10-1. Penetration Test, 2. Test Authentication

P	E	N	E	T	R	A	T	I	O	N	T	E	S	T	E	W	C
V	U	L	N	E	R	A	B	I	L	I	T	B	D	O	T	E	Y
M	K	E	P	O	P	V	N	M	P	Y	H	E	S	D	H	R	E
D	A	I	S	N	E	S	S	N	O	U	R	E	D	E	I	A	R
A	R	P	S	P	O	O	F	I	N	K	W	R	T	B	C	C	G
T	E	S	T	A	U	T	H	E	N	T	I	C	A	T	I	O	N
T	Q	W	O	T	R	C	A	G	W	M	G	E	F	R	I	E	L
R	E	G	R	E	S	S	I	O	N	T	E	S	T	I	N	Q	G

Exercise 11- 1. Penetration Testing, 2. Insecure Direct Object References (IDOR)

Test Paper

Chapter-5

Web Penetration Testing

Time Duration: 30 Minutes **Maximum Marks: 25**

General Instructions:

1. The question paper consists of 12 questions and is divided into four sections, A, B, C and D.
2. All questions are compulsory.
3. Section A comprises MCQs, Fill in the blanks and True or False carrying one marks each.
4. Section B comprises VSAQs(very short answers questions) carrying two marks each.
5. Section C comprises SAQs(short questions) carrying four marks each.
6. Section D comprises long questions carrying five marks each.

SECTION-A

I. Multiple choice questions: **(1*2=2)**

1. Which of the following is a common vulnerability in web applications that can be exploited through user input?
a) Cross-Site Request Forgery (CSRF)
b) Cross-Site Scripting (XSS)
c) SQL Injection
d) All of the above

2. What is the primary objective of using an OWASP Checklist during penetration testing?
a) To list all available vulnerabilities
b) To ensure that all common vulnerabilities are covered
c) To track user interactions
d) To measure system performance

II. Fill in the blanks: **(1*2=2)**

1. ________ refers to the simulated attack on a web application to identify vulnerabilities that could be exploited by attackers.
2. ________ is the vulnerability that occurs when an application exposes references to internal objects without proper access controls.

III. True or False: **(1*2=2)**

1. Hidden Web Contents are files and directories directly visible to users through navigation menus.
2. API Testing involves verifying the security of application programming interfaces to ensure proper Data handling and access control.

SECTION-B

IV. Very Short answers type questions-I **(2*3=6)**

1. Define Cross-Site Scripting (XSS) and provide an example.
2. What is the significance of session management in web application security?
3. Explain what is meant by privilege escalation in the context of web penetration testing.

SECTION-C

V. Short answers type questions-II **(4*2=8)**

1. Describe the process of testing for SQL Injection vulnerabilities in a web application.
2. How does the OWASP Checklist help in identifying vulnerabilities during penetration testing?

SECTION-D

VI. Long answers type questions **(5*1=5)**

1. Discuss the importance of API testing in web penetration testing and outline the key steps involved in performing effective API security testing.

ONLINE RESOURCES

Practice Paper

Link: https://forms.gle/oxAZjuAMyq5YEUix7

QR Code:

YouTube Video Playlist Link

Link: https://www.youtube.com/playlist?list=PLzlh_31VWEFpQ1P6Rw75QdPfiNpoceI17

QR Code:

Chapter 6 - **Malware Analysis**

In this chapter you will learn about:
Introduction to Malware
Static Analysis Techniques
Dynamic Analysis Techniques
Code Review for Malware Detection
Behavioural Analysis of Malicious Executables
Sandbox Technologies for Malware Analysis
Reverse Engineering Malware
Anti-Reverse Engineering Techniques
Malware Handling Procedures
Automated Malware Analysis

Malware analysis is the process of examining and understanding malicious software (malware) to identify its behavior, capabilities, and potential impact. This field is crucial for cybersecurity, as it helps security professionals defend against, respond to, and mitigate the effects of malware attacks. By analyzing malware, organizations can develop effective strategies for detection, prevention, and response.

6.1 Static Analysis Techniques

Static analysis is a crucial technique in malware analysis that involves examining the malicious code without executing it. This method allows analysts to gain insights into the malware's structure, functionality, and potential threats by inspecting the code and associated files. Here's an overview of the key static analysis techniques used in malware analysis:

1. File Inspection

• Objective: To gather basic information about the malware file, such as its type, size, and properties.
• Techniques:
o File MetaData Examination: Analyzing file attributes such as creation date, modification date, and file hashes (e.g., MD5, SHA-1) to identify known samples and understand the file's origin.
o Magic Number Analysis: Checking the file's magic number (a unique identifier in the file header) to determine its format and type (e.g., executable, PDF, script).

2. Code Analysis

• Objective: To understand the malware's functionality by examining its code and structure.
• Techniques:
o Disassembly: Using tools like IDA Pro or Ghidra to convert binary code into assembly language. This helps analysts understand the instructions and logic used in the malware.
o Decompilation: Converting executable code into a higher-level language (e.g., C or Java) using decompiles. This can make it easier to understand the malware's functionality and algorithms.
o String Analysis: Extracting and examining readable strings within the malware to identify potential indicators of malicious behavior, such as URLs, file paths, or command names.

3. Control Flow Analysis

• Objective: To analyze the control flow of the malware to understand its execution path and decision-making processes.
• Techniques:
o Control Flow Graphs (CFG): Creating visual representations of the malware's execution paths. This helps in identifying loops, conditional branches, and the overall structure of the code.
o Call Graph Analysis: Mapping out the functions and their interactions within the malware to understand how different components communicate and execute.

4. Symbol Analysis

• Objective: To identify symbols (e.g., function names, variables) used in the malware code, which can provide insights into its behavior.
• Techniques:
o Symbol Extraction: Using tools to extract and analyze symbolic information from the malware binary, which can reveal function names, variable names, and imported libraries.

o API Function Analysis: Identifying and examining the API calls made by the malware to understand the system functions it interacts with, which can indicate its capabilities and intentions.

5. Signature-Based Detection

• Objective: To detect known malware samples by matching their characteristics against a Database of known signatures.

• Techniques:

o Hash Matching: Comparing file hashes with those in malware Databases to identify known threats.

o Pattern Matching: Searching for specific byte patterns, strings, or other identifiable characteristics within the malware that match known malware signatures.

6.2 Dynamic Analysis Techniques

Dynamic analysis involves observing the behaviour of malware in a controlled environment while it is running. This approach lets analysts see how the malware interacts with the operating system, network, and other components in real time. Dynamic analysis is essential for understanding malware's full impact and identifying behaviours that may not be evident through static analysis alone. Here are key dynamic analysis techniques used in malware analysis:

1. Sandbox Analysis

• Objective: To execute malware in a controlled, isolated environment to monitor its behaviour without risking actual systems.

• Techniques:

o Automated Sandboxes: Tools like Cuckoo Sandbox or Hybrid Analysis provide automated environments where malware can be executed and monitored for file modifications, registry changes, and network connections.

o Behavioral Monitoring: Observing the malware's actions, including file system changes, process creation, network traffic, and interactions with other applications.

2. Behavioral Analysis

• Objective: To document and analyse the real-time actions and effects of malware on the system.

• Techniques:

o System Call Monitoring: Tracking system calls made by the malware to understand its interactions with the operating system and other software components. Tools like Sysinternals' Process Monitor can be used for this purpose.

o Network Traffic Analysis: Monitoring network activity to identify connections to command-and-control servers, Data exfiltration attempts, or communication with malicious entities. Tools like Wireshark or Fiddler can help analyse network traffic.

3. Process Analysis

• Objective: To examine the processes created or modified by the malware and their impact on the system.

• Techniques:

o Process Monitoring: Observing the creation, termination, and behaviour of processes spawned by the malware. Process Explorer or Process Hacker can be used to track process activity.

o Memory Analysis: Analyzing processes' memory to identify injected code, modifications, or anomalies. Tools like Volatility or Rekall are useful for memory analysis.

4. File System Analysis

• Objective: To detect changes made to the file system by the malware, including new files created, existing files modified, or file deletions.

• Techniques:

o File System Monitoring: Using tools to track file system activities, including file reads, writes, and deletions. Tools like Process Monitor or Sysinternals' Filemon can be used for detailed monitoring.

o Registry Analysis: For Windows systems, analyzing changes made to the system registry by the malware, including new keys or values created, and modifications to existing keys. Tools like Regedit or Regshot can help with this analysis.

6.3 Code Review for Malware Detection

Code review for malware detection involves systematically examining source code or binaries to identify malicious behaviour or vulnerabilities that malware could exploit. This process is essential for understanding the intricacies of how malware functions and for detecting hidden threats that may not be apparent through other analysis techniques. Here's a detailed look at code review techniques specifically tailored for malware detection:

1. Static Code Review

• Objective: To analyse the source code or binary files without executing them, focusing on detecting suspicious or malicious code patterns.
• Techniques:
o Code Inspection: Reviewing code manually or with the help of automated tools to identify anomalies, such as unusual function calls, obfuscated code, or suspicious logic.
o Pattern Matching: Searching for known malicious code patterns or signatures within the code, such as hard-coded IP addresses, domain names, or known exploit techniques.
o Control Flow Analysis: Examining the code's control flow to identify irregularities or obfuscation techniques that may be used to hide malicious behaviour.

2. Dynamic Code Analysis

• Objective: To observe the behaviour of code during execution to detect potentially malicious actions or interactions with the system.
• Techniques:
o Instrumentation: Modifying the code or adding hooks to monitor its execution in real time. This can help identify unauthorised actions or interactions with the operating system.
o Behavioral Profiling: Analyzing the runtime behaviour of the code, including system calls, file operations, and network activity, to detect any malicious actions or anomalies.

3. Reverse Engineering

• Objective: To deconstruct and understand compiled binaries or obfuscated code to reveal the underlying logic and identify malicious components.
• Techniques:
o Disassembly: Using tools like IDA Pro or Ghidra to convert binary code into assembly language for analysis. This helps in understanding the low-level operations of the malware.
o Decompilation: Converting binary code into a higher-level programming language (e.g., C) to make the logic more understandable. Tools such as JEB Decompiler or Hex-Rays can be used.
o Code Reconstruction: Rebuilding obfuscated or packed code to uncover its proper functionality and detect hidden malicious behavior.

4. Library and Dependency Analysis

• Objective: To review the libraries and dependencies used by the code to identify any associated malicious activities or vulnerabilities.
• Techniques:
o Library Examination: Checking for the inclusion of suspicious or unknown libraries that could be used to exploit system functions or hide malicious activities.
o Dependency Analysis: Mapping out the code's dependencies and examining their origins and behaviours to ensure they do not introduce vulnerabilities or malicious components.

5. Code Obfuscation Detection

• Objective: To identify techniques that obscure the code's true intent and functionality, making it harder to analyse.
• Techniques:
o Obfuscation Pattern Recognition: Detecting standard obfuscation techniques such as code encryption, function renaming, or control flow alteration that may be used to hide malicious behaviour.
o Deobfuscation: Applying techniques to reverse obfuscation and make the code more readable and understandable. This may involve manual efforts or the use of specialised tools.

6.4 Behavioral Analysis of Malicious Executables

Behavioural analysis of malicious executables focuses on observing and documenting the actions and interactions of malware while it is running. This approach provides insights into the malware's functionality and potential impact, which are critical for understanding how it operates and for developing effective defences. Here's an overview of the essential techniques and processes involved in behavioural analysis:

1. Setting Up a Controlled Environment

• Objective: To create a safe and isolated environment where the malware can be executed and analysed without risking actual systems or Data.
• Techniques:
o Virtual Machines (VMs): Using virtual environments (e.g., VMware, VirtualBox) to run the malware, allowing for easy snapshots and rollback in case of issues.

o Sandboxes: Utilizing specialised sandboxing solutions (e.g., Cuckoo Sandbox, Any. Run) that provide automated and controlled environments for malware execution and behaviour monitoring.

2. Monitoring System Calls

• Objective: To track and analyse the system calls made by the malware, revealing how it interacts with the operating system.

• Techniques:

o System Call Logging: Using tools like Sysinternals' Process Monitor or Strake to log system calls made by the malware, including file operations, registry changes, and network activities.

o Call Analysis: Reviewing the logged system calls to identify patterns or actions indicative of malicious behaviour, such as unauthorised file access or modification.

3. Observing File System Changes

• Objective: To detect and document any malware modifications to the file system.

• Techniques:

o File System Monitoring: Using tools like Process Monitor or Windows Sysinternals' tools to track the malware's file creation, modification, and deletion operations.

o Change Analysis: Analyzing the observed changes to identify malicious actions, such as the creation of hidden files, alteration of system files, or installation of additional payloads.

4. Network Activity Analysis

• Objective: To monitor and analyse network communications initiated by the malware, revealing potential Data exfiltration or command-and-control activities.

• Techniques:

o Network Traffic Monitoring: Using tools like Wire shark or tcpdump to capture and analyse malware-generated network traffic, including connections to external servers and Data transmission.

o DNS and HTTP Requests Analysis: Tracking DNS queries and HTTP requests made by the malware to identify connections to command-and-control servers or other malicious endpoints.

5. Behavioral Profiling

• Objective: To create a detailed profile of the malware's behaviour, including its impact on the system and interactions with other processes.

• Techniques:

o Process Behavior Analysis: Monitoring the creation and termination of processes and interactions between processes to understand the malware's operation and potential impact.

o Registry Changes: Observing modifications to the system registry (on Windows) to detect changes that could indicate persistence mechanisms or configuration alterations.

6.5 Sandbox Technologies for Malware Analysis

Behavioural analysis of malicious executables focuses on observing and documenting the actions and interactions of malware while it is running. This approach provides insights into the malware's functionality and potential impact, which are critical for understanding how it operates and developing effective defences. Here's an overview of the essential techniques and processes involved in behavioural analysis:

1. Setting Up a Controlled Environment

• Objective: To create a safe and isolated environment where the malware can be executed and analysed without risking actual systems or Data.

• Techniques:

o Virtual Machines (VMs): Using virtual environments (e.g., VMware, VirtualBox) to run the malware, allowing for easy snapshots and rollback in case of issues.

o Sandboxes: Utilizing specialised sandboxing solutions (e.g., Cuckoo Sandbox, Any. Run) that provide automated and controlled environments for malware execution and behaviour monitoring.

2. Monitoring System Calls

• Objective: To track and analyse the system calls made by the malware, revealing how it interacts with the operating system.

• Techniques:

o System Call Logging: Using tools like Sysinternals' Process Monitor or Strake to log system calls made by the malware, including file operations, registry changes, and network activities.

o Call Analysis: Reviewing the logged system calls to identify patterns or actions indicative of malicious behaviour, such as unauthorised file access or modification.

3. Observing File System Changes

• Objective: To detect and document any malware modifications to the file system.
• Techniques:
o File System Monitoring: Using tools like Process Monitor or Windows Sysinternals' tools to track the malware's file creation, modification, and deletion operations.
o Change Analysis: Analyzing the observed changes to identify malicious actions, such as the creation of hidden files, alteration of system files, or installation of additional payloads.

4. Network Activity Analysis

• Objective: To monitor and analyse network communications initiated by the malware, revealing potential Data exfiltration or command-and-control activities.
• Techniques:
o Network Traffic Monitoring: Using tools like Wire shark or tcpdump to capture and analyze malware-generated network traffic, including connections to external servers and Data transmission.
o DNS and HTTP Requests Analysis: Tracking DNS queries and HTTP requests made by the malware to identify connections to command-and-control servers or other malicious endpoints.

5. Behavioral Profiling

• Objective: To create a detailed profile of the malware's behaviour, including its impact on the system and interactions with other processes.
• Techniques:
o Process Behavior Analysis: Monitoring the creation and termination of processes and interactions between processes to understand the malware's operation and potential impact.
o Registry Changes: Observing modifications to the system registry (on Windows) to detect changes that could indicate persistence mechanisms or configuration alterations.

6.6 Glossary

• Automated Sandboxes: Pre-configured environments that execute malware and provide detailed analysis reports without manual intervention. Examples include Cuckoo Sandbox and Any. Run.
• Cloud-Based Sandboxes: Sandbox solutions hosted over the internet offer scalability and ease of access for malware analysis. Examples include Virus Total and Hybrid Analysis.
• Interactive Sandboxes: Sandbox environments allow analysts to interact with and control the malware during execution manually. Examples include FireEye Sandbox and Joe Sandbox.
• Isolation: The process of separating malware execution from the host system to prevent any harm or interference. This is achieved using virtual machines or container technologies.
• Network Simulation: The ability of a sandbox to mimic network environments to observe how malware communicates with external servers and performs network activities.
• On-Premises Sandboxes: Sandbox solutions deployed within an organisation's infrastructure, providing greater control and customisation. Examples include Last Line Enterprise.
• Snapshot and Rollback: The ability to capture and restore the state of the sandbox before and after malware execution, facilitating easy clean-up and analysis.
• Sandbox: A secure, isolated environment used to execute and analyse potentially harmful software safely.
• System Call Logging: Tracking and recording system calls made by malware to understand its interactions with the operating system.
• Behavioural Monitoring: Observing and documenting the actions and interactions of malware within a sandbox environment to understand its behaviour and impact.
• Dynamic Analysis: Analyzing malware by executing it and observing its behaviour in a controlled environment, as opposed to static analysis, which examines the code without execution.
• Virtual Machines (VMs): Software-based emulations of physical computers used to create isolated environments for running and analysing malware.

6.7 Summary

1. Static Analysis Techniques

Static analysis involves examining malware without executing it, focusing on code structure, file characteristics, and metaData. Key techniques include:
Disassembly: Converting binary code to assembly language to understand low-level operations.
Decompilation: Translating binaries to higher-level languages for more straightforward interpretation.
String Analysis: Searching for readable strings in binaries to identify potential malicious components.

Static Code Analysis Tools: Utilizing tools like IDA Pro and Ghidra to analyse code structures and detect suspicious patterns.

Static analysis is useful for uncovering embedded Data and understanding the malware's purpose without running it, but it may not reveal dynamic behaviours or interactions with the system.

2. Dynamic Analysis Techniques

Dynamic analysis involves executing malware in a controlled environment to observe its behaviour. Key techniques include:

Execution Monitoring: Observing runtime behaviour such as system calls, file operations, and network activity.

Behavioral Profiling: Creating a profile of the malware's activities and impact on the system.

Dynamic Analysis Tools: Using tools like Process Monitor and Wireshark to capture and analyse real-time Data.

Dynamic analysis provides insights into how malware interacts with the system, revealing behaviours that static analysis may miss. However, it requires a controlled environment to prevent harm.

3. Code Review for Malware Detection

Code review involves examining source code or binaries to identify malicious behaviour. Key techniques include:

Static Code Review: Analyzing code manually or with tools to detect anomalies and malicious patterns.

Reverse Engineering: Deconstruct binaries to understand the underlying logic and detect hidden threats.

Library and Dependency Analysis: Reviewing libraries and dependencies for vulnerabilities or malicious components.

Code review helps understand the malware's inner workings and detect hidden threats, but it can be time-consuming and require expertise in programming and reverse engineering.

4. Behavioral Analysis of Malicious Executables

Behavioural analysis involves observing and documenting the actions of malware during execution. Key aspects include:

Controlled Environment: Using virtual machines or sandboxes to run malware and observe its behaviour safely.

System Call Logging: Tracking system calls to understand interactions with the operating system.

Network Activity Monitoring: Capturing and analysing network traffic to detect communication with external servers.

Behavioural analysis provides a comprehensive view of how malware operates and interacts with its environment, which is essential for understanding its impact and developing countermeasures.

5. Sandbox Technologies for Malware Analysis

Sandbox technologies provide controlled environments for executing and analysing malware safely. Key features and types include:

- Isolation: Preventing malware from affecting the host system.
- Behavioral Monitoring: Tracking actions such as file changes and network activity.
- Automated Sandboxes: Solutions like Cuckoo Sandbox that provide automated reports.
- Interactive Sandboxes: Tools like FireEye Sandbox allow manual control and investigation.
- Cloud-Based Sandboxes: Services like Virus Total offer scalable analysis.
- On-Premises Sandboxes: Solutions like Last Line Enterprise provide customizable environments.

6.8 Previous Year Solved Questions

Question. How do sandbox technologies enhance the process of malware analysis, and what are the key features, types, and challenges associated with their use? (Delhi University, 2021 MCA)

Answer. Sandbox technologies are instrumental in malware analysis, providing controlled, isolated environments where malicious software can be executed and studied safely. These environments enable analysts to observe and understand malware behaviour without risking actual systems or Data, making them crucial in identifying and mitigating threats.

Enhancement of Malware Analysis Process:

1. Controlled Environment: Sandboxes offer a secure space where malware can run without affecting the host system. This isolation ensures that any malicious actions performed by the malware, such as file modifications or network communications, are contained within the sandbox and do not impact the actual system.
2. Behavioural Observation: By executing malware in a sandbox, analysts can monitor its actions, such as system calls, file system changes, and network activity. This detailed observation helps in understanding how the malware operates, what files it interacts with, and how it communicates with external servers.
3. Automated and Interactive Analysis: Many sandbox solutions provide automated analysis features, streamlining the process by generating detailed reports on malware behaviour without manual intervention. Additionally, interactive

sandboxes allow analysts to manually control and interact with the malware, offering more profound insights into its functionality.

Key Features of Sandbox Technologies:

1. Isolation: Sandboxes use virtual machines or container technologies to isolate the malware from the host system. This separation prevents any potential harm or interference from the malware, ensuring that the analysis does not compromise the actual environment.
2. Behavioural Monitoring: Sandboxes track various aspects of malware behaviour, including system calls, file modifications, and network interactions. This monitoring provides comprehensive Data on how the malware operates and its impact on the system.
3. Network Simulation: Sandboxes can simulate network environments to observe how malware communicates with external servers, sends Data, or performs network-based attacks. This feature helps identify command-and-control mechanisms and data exfiltration tactics.
4. Snapshot and Rollback: Sandboxes capture the system's state before and after malware execution, allowing for easy rollback and clean-up. This capability ensures that the sandbox can be quickly restored to a clean state for further analysis.

Types of Sandboxes:

1. Automated Sandboxes: These solutions include Cuckoo Sandbox and Any. Run and execute malware samples and provide automated reports on their behaviour. They are efficient for processing large volumes of samples and quickly generating insights.
2. Interactive Sandboxes: Examples include FireEye Sandbox and Joe Sandbox, which offer manual interaction capabilities. Analysts can control the execution of malware, perform in-depth investigations, and observe real-time behaviour.
3. Cloud-Based Sandboxes: Services like Virus Total and Hybrid Analysis operate over the internet, offering scalable and accessible solutions for malware analysis. These sandboxes provide extensive analysis capabilities and are suitable for handling large-scale malware threats.
4. On-Premises Sandboxes: Deployed within an organisation's infrastructure, solutions like Last Line Enterprise offer greater control and customisation. These sandboxes are tailored to specific organisational needs and provide in-depth analysis capabilities.

Challenges Associated with Sandbox Technologies:

1. Evasion Techniques: Some malware is designed to detect sandbox environments and alter its behaviour to avoid detection. Analysts must be aware of these evasion techniques and use advanced methods to counteract them.
2. Performance Overhead: Running malware in a sandbox may introduce performance issues or affect the accuracy of behavioural observations. Analysts need to account for this overhead and ensure reliable analysis results.
3. Integration Needs: Effective use of sandboxes often requires integration with other analysis tools and processes. Combining sandbox analysis with static analysis, reverse engineering, and other methods provides a more comprehensive understanding of malware.

Exercises

Exercise 1 – Multiple Choice Questions

1. Which of the following is an example of an automated sandbox?
   a)Any. Run
   b)Virus Total
   c)Fire Eye Sandbox
   d)Process Monitor

2. What is the main function of network simulation in a sandbox?
   a) Isolate the malware
   b) Observe malware's network activities
   c) Monitor file changes
   d) Capture and restore system state

Exercise 2 – True/False

1. On-premises sandboxes are deployed in the cloud for easier scalability.

2. System call logging helps in understanding the interaction of malware with the operating system.

Exercise 3 – Fill in the blanks

1. ________ is the ability to capture and restore the state of the sandbox before and after malware execution.
2. A secure, isolated environment used to execute potentially harmful software is known as a ________.

Exercise 4- Fill in the blanks with two options

1. ________ (Dynamic/Static) analysis involves executing malware to observe its behaviour in real-time.
2. Virtual machines are ________ (software-based/hardware-based) emulations of physical computers.

Exercise 5- Rearrange the sentence

1. Analysis/track/to/used/system/calls/is/logging/system.
2. Sandboxes/allow/malware/for/manual/control/interactive.

Exercise 6- Choose the Odd One Out

1. a. Cuckoo Sandbox
b. Last line Enterprise
c. FireEye Sandbox
d. Process Monitor
2. a. Disassembly
b. Decompilation
c. System Call Logging
d. String Analysis

Exercise 7- Jumble words

1. ORTLUVAIMA NICHAMSNEES – ________
2. YNAASMBODX – ________

Exercise 8- Match case

1. Automated Sandbox
2. Cloud-Based Sandbox
3. Interactive Sandbox
4. Isolation

a) A sandbox that allows manual interaction with malware
b) A sandbox hosted over the internet
c) A sandbox that generates analysis reports without manual intervention
d) The process of separating malware from the host system

Exercise 9- Assertion – Reason

1. Assertion: Network simulation is crucial in malware analysis.
Reason: It allows analysts to observe how malware interacts with external servers.
a) Both Assertion and Reason are correct and Reason is the correct explanation for Assertion.
b) Both Assertion and Reason are correct but Reason is not the correct explanation for Assertion.
c) Assertion is correct but Reason is incorrect.
d) Assertion is incorrect but Reason is correct.

2. Assertion: Static analysis can uncover dynamic malware behaviours.
Reason: Static analysis only examines the code without execution.
a) Both Assertion and Reason are correct and Reason is the correct explanation for Assertion.
b) Both Assertion and Reason are correct but Reason is not the correct explanation for Assertion.
c) Assertion is correct but Reason is incorrect.
d) Assertion is incorrect but Reason is correct.

Exercise 10- Read the questions given below and find the appropriate word in the grid provided.

Questions:

1. The technique involving examining malware by converting binary code to assembly language and translating binaries to higher-level languages is known as __________.
2. The process of executing malware in a controlled environment to observe its behavior, including system calls and network activity, is referred to as __________.

Grid:

S	T	A	T	I	C	A	N	A	L	Y	S	I	S	V
V	U	L	N	E	R	A	B	I	L	I	T	B	D	O
S	K	E	P	O	P	V	N	M	P	Y	H	E	S	D
D	Y	N	A	M	I	C	A	N	A	L	Y	S	I	S
A	R	P	S	P	O	O	F	I	N	K	W	R	T	B
R	E	G	R	E	S	S	I	O	N	T	E	S	T	I

Exercise 11- One- word

1. What term describes the process of separating malware execution from the host system?
2. Name the tool used for dynamic analysis of malware.

Exercise 12- Small Answers

1. What is the difference between static and dynamic analysis in malware analysis?
2. How does behavioural monitoring help in understanding malware?

Exercise 13- Long Answers

1. Explain how sandbox technologies are used in malware analysis. Include examples of different types of sandboxes.
2. Describe the steps involved in behavioural analysis of malicious executables.

Exercise 14- Previous Year Unsolved Questions

1. Explain the importance of dynamic analysis in identifying malware behaviours. (Mumbai University, January 2023, MCA)
2. How does reverse engineering assist in malware detection? (Mumbai University, January 2023, MCA)
3. Attempt any FOUR.

a) Explain how criminals plan attack
b) Explain various security challenges posed by mobile devices
c) Explain need of cyber law in India
d) Explain E-contracts and its different types. (Mumbai University, December 2023, MCA)

4. What is meant by Cryptography? Discuss RSA algorithm. (IGNOU, December 2021, MCA)
5. Discuss the issues arising due to Linking, In lining, and Framing. (IGNOU, June 2022, MCA)
6. Discuss in brief the various Data security measures. (IGNOU, June 2022, MCA)

Answers

Exercise 1- 1. a. Any. Run, 2. b. Observe malware's network activities
Exercise 2- 1. False, 2. True
Exercise 3- 1. Snapshot and Rollback, 2. Sandbox
Exercise 4- 1. Dynamic, 2. Software-based
Exercise 5- 1. System call logging is used to track analysis, 2.Interactive sandboxes allow manual control for malware.
Exercise 6- 1. d. Process Monitor, 2. c. System Call Logging
Exercise 7- 1. Virtual Machines, 2. Sandbox
Exercise 8- 1– c, 2 – b, 3 – a, 4 – d
Exercise 9- 1. Assertion: True; Reason: True, 2. Assertion: False; Reason: True
Exercise 10- 1. Static Analysis, 2. Dynamic Analysis

S	T	A	T	I	C	A	N	A	L	Y	S	I	S	V
V	U	L	N	E	R	A	B	I	L	I	T	B	D	O
S	K	E	P	O	P	V	N	M	P	Y	H	E	S	D
D	Y	N	A	M	I	C	A	N	A	L	Y	S	I	S
A	R	P	S	P	O	O	F	I	N	K	W	R	T	B
R	E	G	R	E	S	S	I	O	N	T	E	S	T	I

Exercise 11- 1. Isolation, 2. Process Monitor

Test Paper

Chapter-6

Malware Analysis

Time Duration: 30 Minutes **Maximum Marks: 25**

General Instructions:

1. The question paper consists of 12 questions and is divided into four sections, A, B, C and D.
2. All questions are compulsory.
3. Section A comprises MCQs, Fill in the blanks and True or False carrying one marks each.
4. Section B comprises VSAQs(very short answers questions) carrying two marks each.
5. Section C comprises SAQs(short questions) carrying four marks each.
6. Section D comprises long questions carrying five marks each.

SECTION-A

I. Multiple choice questions: **(1*2=2)**

1. Which of the following is an example of an automated sandbox?

a. Any. Run
b. Virus Total
c. FireEye Sandbox
d. Process Monitor

2. What is the main function of network simulation in a sandbox?

a. Isolate the malware
b. Observe malware's network activities
c. Monitor file changes
d. Capture and restore system state

II. Fill in the blanks: **(1*2=2)**

1. _______ is the ability to capture and restore the state of the sandbox before and after malware execution.
2. A secure, isolated environment used to execute potentially harmful software is known as a _______.

III. True or False: **(1*2=2)**

1. On-premises sandboxes are deployed in the cloud for easier scalability.
2. System call logging helps in understanding the interaction of malware with the operating system.

SECTION-B

IV. Very Short answers type questions-I **(2*3=6)**

1. What is the difference between static and dynamic analysis in malware analysis?
2. Define "Behavioral Monitoring" in the context of sandbox technologies.
3. Explain the concept of "System Call Logging" during malware analysis.

SECTION-C

V. Short answers type questions-II **(4*2=8)**

1. Describe how cloud-based sandboxes operate and give an example.
2. What are the advantages and limitations of using virtual machines for malware analysis?

SECTION-D

VI. Long answers type questions **(5*1=5)**

1. Explain the various types of sandbox technologies used for malware analysis. Discuss their key features and give relevant examples for each type.

ONLINE RESOURCES

Practice Paper
Link: https://forms.gle/42xzEK7kVwYZr7uf9
QR Code:

YouTube Video Playlist Link
Link: https://www.youtube.com/playlist?list=PLzlh_31VWEFqiHFI-CMpCxfkd5OTd5Mto
QR Code:

Chapter 7 - Cyber Crime Investigation

In this chapter you will learn about:
Basics of Cyber Crime Investigation
Cognizance of Cyber Crime
Power of Police Officers in Cyber Crimes
Cyber Forensics Fundamentals
Compoundable Offences (Section 77A)

Cyber crime investigation encompasses the process of identifying, analyzing, and addressing criminal activities conducted through digital means. With the proliferation of internet-based crimes, such as hacking, identity theft, and cyber fraud, investigators need specialized knowledge and tools to track, analyze, and prosecute these offenses. This chapter provides an in-depth exploration of the methodologies, tools, and challenges involved in cybercrime investigation, focusing on the following:

7.1 Basics of Cyber Crime Investigation

The basics of Cyber Crime Investigation involve fundamental concepts and steps required to effectively detect, analyze, and address crimes conducted through digital means. Here's an overview:

- Definition: Cyber crime investigation involves identifying, analyzing, and resolving crimes that occur via computers, networks, or digital devices.
- Types of Cyber Crimes:
    - o Hacking: Unauthorized access to systems or networks.
    - o Identity Theft: Stealing personal information to commit fraud.
    - o Cyber Fraud: Deceptive schemes conducted online for financial gain.
    - o Data Breaches: Unauthorized access or exposure of sensitive Data.
- Initial Steps:
    - o Incident Identification: Detecting signs of a potential cybercrime using monitoring tools and security alerts.
    - o Evidence Preservation: Securing digital evidence to prevent alteration or loss, often involving procedures such as imaging drives and securing logs.
- Tools and Techniques:
    - o Digital Forensics Tools: These are applications for analysing digital evidence, such as EnCase, FTK, and Autopsy.
    - o Network Monitoring Tools: Software to capture and analyse network traffic, like Wireshark and Splunk.
- Investigation Process:
    - o Evidence Collection: Gathering Data from affected systems, logs, network devices, and digital storage.
    - o Analysis: Investigating collected evidence to trace activity, identify perpetrators, and determine the impact.
    - o Reporting: Documenting findings, methodologies, and evidence in detailed reports for legal proceedings and organisational review.
- Legal and Ethical Considerations:
    - o Legal Framework: Adhering to relevant laws and regulations related to digital evidence and cyber crimes.
    - o Ethical Practices: Conducting investigations with respect for privacy and ensuring compliance with legal standards.

7.2 Cognizance of Cyber Crime

Cognizance of Cyber Crime involves understanding the nature, scope, and impact of cyber crimes and the strategies for awareness and prevention. Here's a summary of key points:

- Understanding Cyber Crime:
    - a. Nature: Cyber crimes involve illegal activities conducted through or involving computers and digital networks.
    - b. Scope: Includes a wide range of offences such as hacking, online fraud, identity theft, and cyber espionage.
- Common Types of Cyber Crimes:
    - a. Phishing: Fraudulent attempts to obtain sensitive information by disguising it as a trustworthy entity.
    - b. Ransomware: Malicious software that encrypts Data and demands a ransom for decryption.
    - c. Malware: Software designed to disrupt, damage, or gain unauthorised access to systems.

d. DDoS Attacks: Distributed Denial of Service attacks that overwhelm a system with traffic to render it inoperable.

- Recognizing Indicators:
  - a. Unusual Activity: Signs such as unexpected system slowdowns, unauthorised access attempts, or unusual network traffic.
  - b. Suspicious Communications: Emails or messages that request sensitive information or contain links to unfamiliar sites.
- Prevention Strategies:
  - a. Education and Training: Providing awareness and training to employees and individuals about cyber threats and safe practices.
  - b. Security Measures: Implementing robust security protocols such as firewalls, antivirus software, and regular system updates.
  - c. Incident Response Planning: Developing and maintaining an incident response plan to effectively address and mitigate cyber incidents.
- Legal and Regulatory Framework:
  - a. Cyber Crime Laws: Familiarity with laws and regulations that govern cybercrime and digital evidence handling.
  - b. Compliance Requirements: Adhering to industry standards and legal requirements for Data protection and security.
- Impact of Cyber Crime:
  - a. Financial Losses: Direct theft, fraud, and damage costs.
  - b. Reputation Damage: Harm to an organisation's or individual's reputation following a breach or attack.
  - c. Operational Disruption: Interruptions in business operations due to cyber incidents.

7.3 Power of Police Officers in Cyber Crimes

Power of Police Officers in Cyber Crimes refers to law enforcement officials' authority and capabilities to investigate, prevent, and respond to cyber crimes. Here are key points:

• Authority:

Legal Power: Ability to execute search warrants, seize digital evidence, and arrest suspects involved in cyber crimes.

Jurisdiction: Authority to investigate cyber crimes within their geographical and legal boundaries, which may extend across regions or countries through cooperation with other agencies.

• Investigation Capabilities:

Digital Evidence Collection: Authority to collect and preserve digital evidence from computers, networks, and mobile devices in accordance with legal procedures.

Forensic Analysis: Power to use forensic tools and techniques to analyse digital evidence and uncover relevant information.

• Coordination and Collaboration:

Interagency Cooperation: Ability to work with other law enforcement agencies, cybersecurity firms, and international organisations to address complex cybercrime cases.

Public and Private Sector Partnerships: Collaboration with private entities and organisations to share information, resources, and expertise.

• Enforcement Actions:

Prosecutorial Support: Assisting in preparing cases for prosecution by providing evidence and expert testimony.

Cyber Crime Units: Specialized units within police forces dedicated to handling cyber crimes, equipped with advanced tools and trained personnel.

• Challenges and Limitations:

Technical Expertise: Specialised knowledge and skills are needed to effectively investigate and respond to cyber crimes.

Legal Constraints: Adhering to legal and procedural requirements while conducting investigations to ensure evidence is admissible in court.

Resource Allocation: Managing limited resources and prioritising cases based on severity and impact.

7.4 Cyber Forensics Fundamentals

Cyber Forensics Fundamentals involve the principles and practices of investigating digital crimes and gathering evidence from electronic devices. Here are the key points:

Compoundable Offences (Section 77A)

• Definition: Cyber Forensics: The process of collecting, preserving, analysing, and presenting digital evidence from computers, networks, and digital storage devices in a manner suitable for legal proceedings.
• Key Principles:
Adherence to Legal Standards: Ensuring that all forensic activities comply with legal and procedural guidelines to maintain the integrity and admissibility of evidence.
Chain of Custody: Documenting every step of evidence handling to ensure that the evidence remains unaltered and its authenticity is preserved.
• Processes:
o Evidence Collection: Acquiring digital evidence forensically soundly, using tools and techniques to prevent Data alteration. This includes imaging drives and capturing volatile Data (e.g., RAM).
o Evidence Preservation: Protecting collected Data from modification or corruption. This involves using write-blockers and secure storage solutions.
o Data Analysis: Examining digital evidence to identify, recover, and analyse relevant information. Techniques include file recovery, metadata analysis, and network traffic analysis.
o Reporting: Documenting findings in a clear and comprehensive manner, often including expert testimony in legal settings.
• Tools and Techniques:
o Forensic Software: Specialized tools like EnCase, FTK, and X1 for Data recovery, analysis, and reporting.
o Hardware Tools: Devices such as write-blockers and forensic duplicators to ensure the integrity of evidence during collection.
• Types of Digital Evidence:
o File Systems: Analysis of file structures, metadata, and hidden files.
o Network Logs: Examine network traffic and communication logs to trace activities and interactions.
o Emails and Communications: Recovery and analysis of email correspondence and other digital communications.

Compoundable Offences (Section 77A) refers to a specific legal framework for resolving certain offences through an agreement between the parties involved. Here are the key points:
• Definition: Compoundable Offences: Crimes that can be resolved through mutual agreement between the accused and the victim, allowing the offence to be withdrawn or settled outside of court.
• Legal Framework: Section 77A: A specific provision in legal statutes (e.g., some jurisdictions' criminal procedure codes) that outlines the conditions under which certain offences may be compounded.
• Key Features:
o Consent: The process typically requires the consent of both the victim and the accused to resolve the matter.
o Court Approval: In many cases, the court must approve the agreement to ensure it meets legal requirements and is fair to all parties involved.
o Types of Offences: Generally includes minor or less severe offences that do not significantly threaten public safety.
• Procedure:
o Filing a Petition: The parties involved may need to file a petition with the court requesting the offence to be compounded.
o Agreement: An agreement is reached between the parties, outlining the terms of the settlement or resolution.
o Court Hearing: The court reviews and approves the agreement, ensuring it is legally sound.
• Advantages:
o Reduced Litigation: Allows for a quicker resolution and potentially reduces the need for prolonged court proceedings.
o Restorative Justice: Provides an opportunity for the parties to reach a mutually acceptable resolution, which may include restitution or compensation.

7.4 Cybercrime Investigation Tools

Cybercrime Investigation Tools have specialised software and hardware law enforcement and cybersecurity professionals use to detect, analyse, and resolve cyber crimes. Here are the key points:
• Digital Forensics Tools:
EnCase: Comprehensive software for Data acquisition, analysis, and reporting.
FTK (Forensic Toolkit): Provides capabilities for disk imaging, Data recovery, and detailed forensic analysis.
Autopsy: An open-source tool for digital forensics that is used to examine hard drives, analyse file systems, and recover data.

• Network Analysis Tools:
Wireshark: Network protocol analyser for capturing and inspecting network traffic.
NetFlow: Monitors and analyses network flow Data to identify suspicious activities.
Splunk: Provides real-time Data collection, indexing, and analysis for network security.
• Malware Analysis Tools:
Cuckoo Sandbox: Automated malware analysis tool that runs suspicious files in a controlled environment.
VirusTotal: Online service that analyses files and URLs for viruses and malware using multiple antivirus engines.
PEiD: Detects packers, cryptors, and compilers used to obfuscate malware.
• Data Recovery Tools:
R-Studio: File recovery software capable of retrieving Data from damaged or corrupted storage devices.
Recuva: Utility for recovering lost files from hard drives, memory cards, and other storage devices.
• Password Cracking Tools:
John the Ripper: Password cracking software that supports various encryption algorithms and hash types.
Hash cat: Advanced password recovery tool that uses GPU acceleration to crack hashed passwords.
• Email Analysis Tools:
MailXaminer: Specialized tool for analysing email Data, including recovery, extraction, and examination of email artefacts.
Forensic Email Collector: Captures and processes email Data for forensic investigation.
• Incident Response Tools:
The Hive: Open-source incident response platform for managing and analysing security incidents.
Cortex: Complementary to The Hive, it automates the analysis of security incidents and provides actionable insights.
• Legal and Compliance Tools:
X1 Social Discovery: Tool for collecting and analysing Data from social media platforms and web sources for investigative purposes.
FTK Imager: Used for creating forensic images of digital evidence while preserving its integrity.

7.5 Digital Evidence Collection

Digital Evidence Collection involves the systematic process of identifying, acquiring, and preserving digital Data from electronic devices and systems for use in investigations and legal proceedings. Key points include:
Definition: **Digital Evidence**: Information stored or transmitted in digital form that can be used to prove or disprove elements of a crime or incident.
• Collection Process:
o Identification: Determining which devices and Data sources (e.g., computers, mobile devices, servers) are relevant to the investigation.
o Acquisition: Gathering digital evidence forensically sound to avoid alteration or loss of Data. Techniques include:
a. Imaging: Creating an exact bit-by-bit copy of digital storage media (e.g., hard drives) to work from a replica rather than the original.
b. Live Data Collection: Capturing volatile Data such as RAM and active processes, which can be lost if the system is powered off.
o Preservation: Ensuring that the integrity of the collected evidence is maintained. This includes:
a. Using Write-Blockers: Devices that prevent modification of the original Data during the imaging process.
b. Secure Storage: Storing evidence in a controlled environment to prevent unauthorised access or tampering.
• Tools and Techniques:
o Forensic Imaging Tools: Software like EnCase, FTK Imager, and hardware devices that create exact copies of digital evidence.
o Data Recovery Tools: Utilities such as R-Studio and Recuva are used to retrieve lost or deleted files.
o Network Capture Tools: Software like Wireshark for capturing network traffic and logs.
• Documentation and Chain of Custody:
o Chain of Custody: Documenting each step of evidence handling to track who collected, transferred, or analysed the evidence to ensure its credibility.
o Detailed Records: Keeping logs of the evidence collection process, including date, time, methods used, and any actions taken.
• Legal and Ethical Considerations:
o Compliance with Laws: Adhering to legal standards and regulations regarding evidence collection, such as obtaining proper warrants and respecting privacy laws.

o Ethical Practices: Ensuring evidence is collected and handled in a manner that respects individual rights and maintains the investigation's integrity.

7.6 Chain of Custody in Cyber Crime Investigations

Chain of Custody refers to the process of maintaining and documenting the handling of evidence from the moment it is collected until it is presented in court. It is crucial in cybercrime investigations to ensure that digital evidence remains credible and unaltered. Key points include:

• **Definition:**

o **Chain of Custody:** The chronological documentation of who collected, handled, transferred, or analysed evidence. It is crucial for establishing the integrity and authenticity of evidence.

• **Importance:**

o **Evidence Integrity:** Ensures that the evidence presented in court is the same as what was originally collected.

o **Admissibility:** Proper documentation helps meet legal requirements for evidence to be admissible in court.

o **Preventing Tampering:** Provides a clear record that can be used to demonstrate that evidence has not been altered or compromised.

• **Key Steps:**

o **Evidence Collection:** Documenting who collected the evidence, when, and using what methods.

o **Handling:** Recording all individuals who come into contact with the evidence and their actions.

o **Transfer:** Keeping detailed logs of evidence transfers between individuals or locations.

o **Analysis:** Recording who analyses the evidence and the techniques used during the analysis.

• **Documentation:**

o **Chain of Custody Log:** A formal record detailing each person who handled the evidence, including dates, times, and descriptions of their actions.

o **Evidence Labels:** Tags or labels attached to evidence items that include identification numbers, collection dates, and collector information.

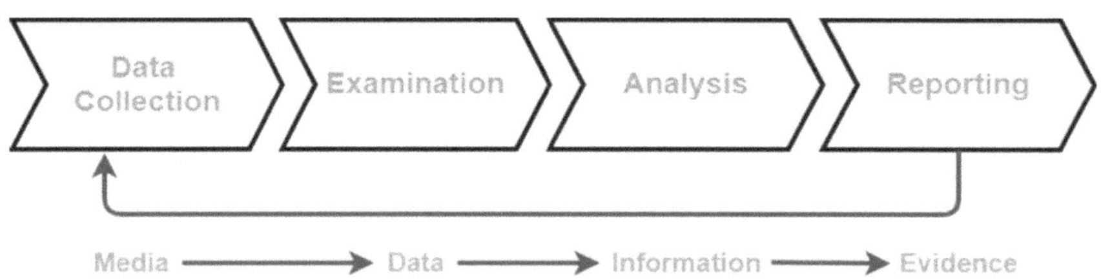

7.7 Reporting and Documentation in Cyber Crime Cases

Reporting and Documentation in cybercrime cases involve creating detailed records and reports that capture the findings of an investigation, the procedures followed, and the evidence collected. This is crucial for legal proceedings and organisational accountability. Key points include:

• **Purpose:**

a. Legal Evidence: Providing a comprehensive investigation account to support legal actions and court proceedings.

b. Organizational Insight: Offering detailed information to help organisations understand the impact of the crime and improve security measures.

• **Types of Documentation:**

a. Incident Reports: Initial reports detailing the discovery of the cybercrime, affected systems, and immediate actions are taken.

b. Chain of Custody Records: Logs documenting the handling and transfer of evidence to ensure its integrity.

c. Forensic Analysis Reports: Detailed descriptions of forensic procedures, tools used, and analysis results, including findings and conclusions.

• **Key Components:**

a. Executive Summary: A high-level overview of the incident, key findings, and recommendations aimed at non-technical stakeholders.

b. Detailed Findings: In-depth analysis of the evidence, including how the crime was committed, the impact, and the identification of perpetrators.

c. Technical Details: Specifics of the technical aspects of the investigation, such as system logs, malware analysis, and network traffic patterns.

d. Evidence Presentation: Clear documentation of the evidence collected, including screenshots, logs, and forensic images.

• **Best Practices:**

a. Clarity and Accuracy: Ensuring reports are clear, precise, and free from jargon to be understood by all relevant parties.

b. Timeliness: Producing reports promptly to ensure that information is relevant and can be acted upon quickly.

c. Consistency: Following standardised formats and procedures to ensure uniformity and completeness in documentation.

7.8 Role of International Cooperation in Cyber Crime Investigations

International Cooperation is crucial in cybercrime investigations due to the global nature of the internet and digital crimes, which often cross national borders. Key points include:

• **Global Reach of Cyber Crimes:**

a. Cross-Border Issues: Cyber crimes often involve perpetrators, victims, or infrastructure located in multiple countries.

b. Jurisdictional Challenges: Different countries have varying laws and regulations, complicating the investigation and prosecution of cyber crimes.

• **Importance of Cooperation:**

a. Information Sharing: Facilitates the exchange of intelligence, evidence, and best practices among countries to combat cyber threats effectively.

b. Resource Utilization: Countries can leverage each other's technological expertise, resources, and tools for more comprehensive investigations.

c. Coordination: Ensures that actions taken in one country complement those in others, avoiding duplication of efforts and enhancing overall effectiveness.

• **Mechanisms of Cooperation:**

a. International Treaties and Agreements: Frameworks like the Council of Europe's Convention on Cybercrime (Budapest Convention) establish guidelines for cooperation and mutual assistance in cybercrime cases.

b. Interpol and Europol: Provide platforms for international law enforcement agencies to collaborate, share information, and coordinate operations against cyber criminals.

c. Mutual Legal Assistance Treaties (MLATs): Formal agreements between countries for requesting and providing assistance in legal matters, including evidence collection and prosecution.

d. Joint Task Forces: Collaborative teams that involve law enforcement, cybersecurity experts, and other stakeholders from multiple countries working together on specific cases or threats.

• **Challenges:**

a. Legal Differences: Variations in laws and regulations across countries can complicate cooperation and affect the admissibility of evidence.

b. Privacy and Data Protection: Balancing international cooperation with the need to protect individual privacy and comply with Data protection laws.

c. Political and Diplomatic Issues: Navigating political or diplomatic tensions that may impact the willingness or ability of countries to cooperate.

7.9 Glossary

1. Basics of Cyber Crime Investigation

    a. Cyber Crime: Criminal activities that involve computers and networks, including hacking, fraud, and identity theft.

    b. Investigation: The process of gathering and analysing information to uncover and address criminal activities.

    c. Digital Evidence: Information stored or transmitted electronically that can be used in a legal investigation.

    d. Cognizance of Cyber Crime

    e. Cognizance: Awareness or acknowledgement of a crime by authorities, triggering the investigation process.

    f. Jurisdiction: The authority of a law enforcement agency to investigate and enforce laws within a specific geographic area.

2. Power of Police Officers in Cyber Crimes

    a. Authority: Legal power granted to police officers to conduct investigations, seize evidence, and make arrests.

b. Chain of Custody: Documentation of evidence handling to ensure its integrity and authenticity throughout the investigation.
c. Cyber Forensics Fundamentals
d. Cyber Forensics: The practice of collecting, analysing, and preserving digital evidence for legal purposes.
e. Forensic Imaging: Creating an exact copy of digital storage media to analyse without altering the original Data.
f. Chain of Custody: The process of tracking and documenting evidence handling.
g. Compoundable Offences (Section 77A)
h. Compoundable Offences: Crimes that can be settled through an agreement between the accused and the victim, often involving the withdrawal or settlement of charges.
i. Section 77A: A legal provision outlining conditions under which certain offences may be compounded.

3. Cybercrime Investigation Tools
    a. EnCase: Forensic software for Data acquisition, analysis, and reporting.
    b. FTK (Forensic Toolkit): Disk imaging and Data recovery software.
    c. Wireshark: Network protocol analyser for capturing and inspecting network traffic.
    d. Cuckoo Sandbox: Automated malware analysis tool.
4. Digital Evidence Collection
    a. Evidence Collection: The process of acquiring digital Data forensically soundly.
    b. Forensic Imaging: Creating exact copies of digital media for analysis.
    c. Write-Blockers: Devices used to prevent alteration of Data during evidence collection.
5. Chain of Custody in Cyber Crime Investigations
    a. Chain of Custody: Detailed documentation of evidence handling, ensuring its integrity and authenticity.
    b. Documentation: Records and logs that track evidence collection, handling, and analysis.
6. Reporting and Documentation in Cyber Crime Cases
    a. Incident Reports: Initial records describing the discovery and response to a cybercrime.
    b. Forensic Analysis Reports: Detailed accounts of forensic procedures and findings.
    c. Executive Summary: A high-level overview of the investigation's results and recommendations.
7. Role of International Cooperation in Cyber Crime Investigations
    a. International Cooperation: Collaboration between countries and international organisations to address cybercrime.
    b. Interpol: International police organisation facilitating cooperation between law enforcement agencies.
    c. Europol: European law enforcement agency supporting combating severe international crime.
    d. Mutual Legal Assistance Treaties (MLATs): Agreements between countries for legal assistance in criminal matters.

7.10 Summary

- Basics of Cyber Crime Investigation This subchapter introduces the fundamental concepts of cybercrime investigations, including the types of criminal activities involving computers and networks, the methods used to uncover these crimes and the role of digital evidence. It emphasises the importance of systematic investigation techniques and the need for technical expertise in dealing with cybercrime.
- Cognizance of Cyber Crime This section covers the legal and procedural aspects of recognising and acknowledging cyber crimes. It explains how authorities become aware of these crimes, the processes involved in initiating investigations, and the challenges associated with jurisdictional issues when crimes span multiple regions.
- Power of Police Officers in Cyber Crimes This subchapter details the legal authority and responsibilities of police officers in cybercrime investigations. It includes the powers granted to law enforcement, such as evidence seizure and arrests, and the importance of maintaining a proper chain of custody to ensure the integrity of the evidence collected.
- Cyber Forensics Fundamentals This section delves into the principles and practices of cyber forensics, focusing on collecting, analysing, and preserving digital evidence. It covers key concepts such as forensic imaging, maintaining the chain of custody, and using specialised tools to handle digital Data effectively.
- Compoundable Offences (Section 77A) Here, the focus is on certain offences that can be resolved through mutual agreement between the accused and the victim, as outlined in Section 77A. It explains the conditions under which these offences can be compounded and the procedural aspects involved in such resolutions.
- Cybercrime Investigation Tools This subchapter provides an overview of the various tools used in cybercrime investigations. It covers forensic software like EnCase and FTK, network analysis tools like Wireshark, and malware analysis tools like Cuckoo Sandbox, highlighting their functions and importance in the investigative process.

• Digital Evidence Collection This section describes the processes involved in collecting digital evidence, including the techniques for evidence acquisition, preservation, and documentation. It emphasises the use of forensic imaging, write-blockers, and secure storage practices to ensure the reliability of the evidence.
• Chain of Custody in Cyber Crime Investigations This subchapter discusses the importance of maintaining a detailed chain of custody for digital evidence. It outlines the procedures for documenting evidence handling, ensuring that all actions are recorded accurately to preserve the evidence's integrity and admissibility in court.
• Reporting and Documentation in Cyber Crime Cases This section focuses on creating reports and documentation for cybercrime cases. It covers the types of reports needed, including incident reports and forensic analysis reports, and highlights best practices for clear, accurate, and timely documentation to support legal and organisational needs.
• Role of International Cooperation in Cyber Crime Investigations The final subchapter explores the role of international cooperation in tackling cybercrime. It discusses the mechanisms for global collaboration, such as international treaties, organisations like Interpol and Europol, and mutual legal assistance treaties. It addresses the challenges and benefits of working across borders to combat cyber threats.

7.11 Previous Year Solved Questions

Question. How does the investigation of cyber crimes integrate various elements such as digital evidence collection, chain of custody, reporting, and international cooperation to effectively address and resolve cases of cyber crime, and what are the key challenges and best practices associated with each of these elements? (Mumbai University, 2022 MCA)

Answer. The investigation of cyber crimes is a complex process that involves several critical components working together to ensure that crimes are effectively addressed and resolved. These components include digital evidence collection, maintaining the chain of custody, reporting and documentation, and international cooperation. Each element plays a crucial role in the overall investigation process and presents unique challenges and best practices.

1. **Digital Evidence Collection**:
   Integration: Collecting digital evidence involves identifying relevant Data from electronic devices and systems, such as computers, mobile devices, and servers. The evidence collected can include files, emails, logs, and network traffic.
   Challenges: One of the main challenges is ensuring that evidence is gathered forensically to avoid altering or losing Data. Other challenges include dealing with encrypted or password-protected Data and managing large volumes of information.
   Best Practices: To address these challenges, investigators use forensic imaging tools to create exact copies of storage media without modifying the original Data. Write-blockers are employed to prevent changes during evidence collection, and secure storage solutions are used to protect the integrity of the evidence.
2. **Chain of Custody**:
   Integration: The chain of custody involves documenting every person who handles evidence and every action taken from collection to presentation in court. This process ensures that the evidence remains unaltered and credible.
   Challenges: Maintaining an accurate chain of custody can be challenging due to the potential for human error and the complexity of handling multiple pieces of digital evidence. Additionally, ensuring that documentation is complete and up-to-date is essential but can be cumbersome.
   Best Practices: Implementing a detailed chain of custody log and standardised procedures for evidence handling can help mitigate these challenges. Regular audits and training for personnel involved in evidence management further enhance the reliability of the chain of custody.
3. **Reporting and Documentation**:
   Integration: Effective reporting and documentation involve creating comprehensive reports that detail the investigation's findings, methodologies, and evidence. These reports are crucial for legal proceedings and organisational understanding.
   Challenges: The complexity of digital data can make it difficult to present findings clearly and understandably. Additionally, there is a need to balance technical detail with accessibility for non-technical stakeholders.
   Best Practices: Using standardised reporting formats and providing clear executive summaries can help address these challenges. Ensuring that documentation is accurate, timely, and well-organized supports both legal and organisational needs.

International Cooperation:

Integration: Cyber crimes often involve actors, victims, or infrastructure across multiple countries, making international cooperation essential. This cooperation includes sharing information, coordinating actions, and leveraging global resources.
Challenges: Jurisdictional differences, varying legal standards, and political or diplomatic issues can complicate international collaboration. Data privacy concerns and differing regulations also pose challenges.
Best Practices: Establishing clear protocols for information sharing and evidence handling, building trust among international partners, and utilising frameworks like the Budapest Convention can facilitate effective cooperation. Training and capacity-building initiatives also play a role in enhancing global collaboration.

Exercises

Exercise 1 – Multiple Choice Questions

1. What is the main purpose of forensic imaging in cyber forensics?
a. To analyze network traffic
b. To create an exact copy of digital storage media
c. To document evidence handling
d. To perform real-time malware analysis

2. Which tool is used for network protocol analysis?
a. EnCase
b. FTK
c. Wireshark
d. Cuckoo Sandbox

Exercise 2 – True/False

1. Digital evidence can only be used in physical crime investigations.
2. Chain of custody is essential for maintaining the integrity of evidence during a cyber crime investigation.

Exercise 3 – Fill in the blanks

1. ________ is the process of creating an exact copy of digital storage media for analysis without altering the original Data.
2. The legal power granted to police officers to conduct investigations and make arrests is referred to as ________.

Exercise 4- Fill in the blanks with two options

1. Cyber Forensics involves ________ (collecting/analyzing) and preserving digital evidence.
2. Write-blockers are used to prevent ________ (alteration/duplication) of Data during evidence collection.

Exercise 5- Rearrange the sentence

1. is/forensic/imaging/making/a/copy/an/exact/creating
2. forensics/cyber/investigation/tools/important/are/essential

Exercise 6- Choose the Odd One Out

1. a. EnCase
b. FTK
c. Virus Total
d. Cuckoo Sandbox
2. a. Digital Evidence
b. Chain of Custody
c. Forensic Imaging
d. Cloud-Based Sandbox

Exercise 7- Jumble words

1. NGTOCAIIRZCEN - ________
2. SUCOINMTARI - ________

Exercise 8- Match case

1. Cyber Forensics
2. Forensic Imaging
3. Chain of Custody
4. Digital Evidence

a) Documentation of evidence handling to ensure integrity
b) Creating an exact copy of digital storage media
c) The practice of collecting, analyzing, and preserving digital evidence
d) Information stored or transmitted electronically

Exercise 9- Assertion – Reason

1. Assertion: The chain of custody is crucial for the integrity of digital evidence.
Reason: It ensures that all handling of evidence is documented and recorded.
a) Both Assertion and Reason are correct and Reason is the correct explanation for Assertion.
b) Both Assertion and Reason are correct but Reason is not the correct explanation for Assertion.
c) Assertion is correct but Reason is incorrect.
d) Assertion is incorrect but Reason is correct.

2. Assertion: International cooperation is not essential for cyber crime investigations.
Reason: Cyber crimes are usually handled within the country where they occur.
a) Both Assertion and Reason are correct and Reason is the correct explanation for Assertion.
b) Both Assertion and Reason are correct but Reason is not the correct explanation for Assertion.
c) Assertion is correct but Reason is incorrect.
d) Assertion is incorrect but Reason is correct.

Exercise 10- Read the questions given below and find the appropriate word in the grid provided.
Questions:

1. The process of collecting, analyzing, and preserving digital evidence is known as __________.
2. The legal authority and responsibilities granted to law enforcement in cyber crime investigations are described as __________.

Grid:

P	H	O	A	I	J	F	J	Q
O	U	L	N	E	R	O	B	I
L	K	E	P	O	P	R	N	M
I	A	I	S	N	E	E	S	N
C	Y	B	E	R	O	N	F	I
E	M	N	O	S	A	S	L	H
P	Q	W	O	T	R	I	A	G
O	E	R	T	Y	U	C	Q	E
W	A	S	D	F	K	S	A	D
E	J	H	G	F	M	I	Z	C
R	E	G	R	E	S	S	I	O

Exercise 11- One- word

1. What term describes the process of creating an exact copy of digital storage media for analysis?
2. Name the network protocol analyzer used in cyber crime investigations.

Exercise 12- Small Answers

1. What is the role of forensic imaging in digital evidence collection?
2. Explain the importance of maintaining a chain of custody in cyber investigations.

Exercise 13- Long Answers

1. Discuss the fundamentals of cyber forensics, including key concepts and practices involved in the collection and analysis of digital evidence.
2. Describe the role and significance of international cooperation in tackling cyber crime, including relevant organizations and agreements.

Exercise 14- Previous Year Unsolved Questions

1. Explain the process and significance of digital evidence collection in cyber crime investigations. (Delhi University, MCA 2022)
2. Discuss the different types of cyber crime investigation tools and their applications in forensic analysis. (Delhi University, MCA 2022)
3. Discuss the core elements of Data security. (IGNOU, December 2021, MCA)
4. Critically examine the copyright issues in digital medium. (IGNOU, December 2021, MCA)
5. Discuss the law in United States for regulation of cyberspace. (IGNOU, December 2021, MCA)

Answers

Exercise 1- 1. b. To create an exact copy of digital storage media, 2. c. Wireshark
Exercise 2- 1. False, 2. True
Exercise 3- 1. Forensic Imaging, 2. Authority
Exercise 4- 1. Analyzing, 2. Alteration
Exercise 5- 1. Creating an exact copy is forensic imaging., 2. Forensics tools are essential for cyber investigation.
Exercise 6- 1. c. Virus Total, 2. d. Cloud-Based Sandbox
Exercise 7- 1. COGNIZANCE, 2. COMPOUNDABLE
Exercise 8- 1- c, 2- b, 3- a, 4- d
Exercise 9- 1. Assertion: The chain of custody is crucial for the integrity of digital evidence.
Reason: It ensures that all handling of evidence is documented and recorded.
(Both Assertion and Reason are correct), 2. Assertion: International cooperation is not essential for cyber crime investigations.
Reason: Cyber crimes are usually handled within the country where they occur.
(Assertion is false; Reason is correct)
Exercise 10- 1.FORENSICS, 2. POLICE POWER

P	H	O	A	I	J	F	J	Q
O	U	L	N	E	R	O	B	I
L	K	E	P	O	P	R	N	M
I	A	I	S	N	E	E	S	N
C	Y	B	E	R	O	N	F	I
E	M	N	O	S	A	S	L	H
P	Q	W	O	T	R	I	A	G
O	E	R	T	Y	U	C	Q	E
W	A	S	D	F	K	S	A	D
E	J	H	G	F	M	I	Z	C
R	E	G	R	E	S	S	I	O

Exercise 11- 1. Forensic Imaging, 2. Wireshark

Test Paper

Chapter-7

Cyber Crime Investigation

Time Duration: 30 Minutes **Maximum Marks: 25**

General Instructions:

1. The question paper consists of 12 questions and is divided into four sections, A, B, C and D.
2. All questions are compulsory.
3. Section A comprises MCQs, Fill in the blanks and True or False carrying one marks each.
4. Section B comprises VSAQs(very short answers questions) carrying two marks each.
5. Section C comprises SAQs(short questions) carrying four marks each.
6. Section D comprises long questions carrying five marks each.

SECTION-A

I. Multiple choice questions: **(1*2=2)**

1. What tool is used for forensic imaging of digital storage media?
a) EnCase
b) FTK
c) Wireshark
d) Cuckoo Sandbox

2. What is the primary purpose of Chain of Custody in cyber crime investigations?
a) To track evidence handling
b) To acquire digital Data
c) To analyze network traffic
d) To create exact copies of digital media

II. Fill in the blanks: **(1*2=2)**

1. __________ is the practice of collecting, analyzing, and preserving digital evidence for legal purposes.
2. __________ involves creating an exact copy of digital storage media to analyze without altering the original Data.

III. True or False: **(1*2=2)**

1. Cyber crimes are typically resolved through local law enforcement agencies without the need for international cooperation.
2. Forensic imaging is a technique used to analyze network traffic.

SECTION-B

IV. Very Short answers type questions-I **(2*3=6)**

1. What is the role of forensic imaging in cyber crime investigations?
2. Name one tool used for network protocol analysis in cyber crime investigations.
3. What is the purpose of write-blockers in digital evidence collection?

SECTION-C

V. Short answers type questions-II **(4*2=8)**

1. Describe the significance of maintaining a Chain of Custody in the context of digital evidence.
2. Explain the difference between automated and interactive sandboxes in malware analysis.

SECTION-D

VI. Long answers type questions **(5*1=5)**

1. Discuss the role of international cooperation in cyber crime investigations, including the mechanisms for global collaboration and the benefits and challenges associated with it.

ONLINE RESOURCES

Practice Paper

Link: https://forms.gle/R1vqhQUiDPspyv2u9

QR Code:

YouTube Video Playlist Link

Link: https://www.youtube.com/playlist?list=PLzlh_31VWEFogPis57wcuY8zrKcVLgpBb

QR Code:

Chapter 8 - Web Authentication and Session Management

In this chapter you will learn about:
Basics of Web Authentication
Two-factor and Three-factor Authentication
Securing Password-based Authentication
Securing Web Authentication Mechanisms
Authorization Fundamentals
Types of Permissions in Web Applications
Time of Check to Time of Use (TOCTTOU) Exploits

Web authentication and session management are critical components of web application security, ensuring that only authorized users can access certain resources and that user sessions are securely managed throughout their interaction with a web application.

• Web Authentication: The process of verifying the identity of a user attempting to access a web application. Common methods include passwords, multi-factor authentication (MFA), and token-based authentication.
• Session Management: Involves creating and maintaining user sessions after authentication, ensuring secure communication between the user and the web application during the session. This includes managing session tokens (such as cookies) and implementing mechanisms to prevent session hijacking, fixation, and timeout vulnerabilities.

8.1 Basics of Web Authentication

Web authentication is the process of verifying a user's identity to allow access to secure areas of a web application. Key points include:

• Username and Password: This is the most common form of authentication, in which users provide a unique combination of credentials to prove their identity.
• Multi-Factor Authentication (MFA): Adds an extra layer of security by requiring two or more forms of verification, such as a password and a one-time code sent to a mobile device.
• Token-Based Authentication: Upon successful login, users receive a token (like a JSON Web Token, JWT), which is stored in the browser and used for subsequent authentication during a session.
• OAuth and SSO (Single Sign-On) are methods that allow users to log in to multiple applications using a single set of credentials, often through third-party providers like Google or Facebook.

Strong authentication practices are essential to protect web applications from unauthorised access and various security threats, such as credential stuffing and brute-force attacks.

8.2 Two-factor and Three-factor Authentication

Two-Factor Authentication (2FA) and **Three-Factor Authentication (3FA)** are advanced security mechanisms that require users to provide multiple verification forms before accessing a web application. These methods enhance security by adding layers beyond traditional password-based systems.

Two-Factor Authentication (2FA)

2FA requires users to provide **two forms of verification** from the following categories:

Something you know: A password or PIN.

Something you have: A physical device, such as a smartphone (for receiving SMS codes, email verification, or authenticator app tokens).

Something you are: Biometric verification, such as fingerprint or facial recognition.

Example: You log in with a password (something you know) and then enter a code sent to your mobile phone (something you have).

Advantages: Reduces the risk of unauthorised access if one factor (like a password) is compromised. Widely used in online banking, email services, and corporate networks.

Challenges: User inconvenience and reliance on the availability of the second factor (like losing access to a phone).

Three-Factor Authentication (3FA)

3FA introduces an additional layer by requiring **three forms of verification**, combining:

Something you know (password/PIN),

Something you have (smartcard, mobile device), and

Something you are (biometric, like iris scan or fingerprint).
Example: Entering a password, inserting a smart card, and scanning a fingerprint for full access.
Advantages: Enhanced security by ensuring multiple independent factors are verified.
Challenges: Complexity in implementation and user inconvenience, especially in environments where specialised hardware (e.g., biometric scanners) is required.

8.3 Securing Password-based Authentication

Password-based authentication remains one of the most common methods for securing access to web applications. Still, it is also highly vulnerable to attacks like brute force, credential stuffing, and phishing. Securing this method requires implementing best practices to protect both user credentials and authentication systems.

Key Strategies for Securing Password-Based Authentication:

1. Strong Password Policies:

1. Enforce the use of complex passwords that include a combination of uppercase and lowercase letters, numbers, and special characters.
2. Set a minimum password length (typically 8–12 characters) to prevent weak password choices.
3. Encourage or require periodic password changes to minimise risks of compromised credentials.

2. Hashing and Salting Passwords:

1. Store passwords using cryptographic hashing algorithms (e.g., bcrypt, Argon2) to transform the plaintext password into a non-reversible hashed value.
2. Salting: Add a unique, random value (salt) to each password before hashing. This prevents attackers from using precomputed hash tables (rainbow tables) to crack passwords.

3. Rate Limiting and Account Lockout:

1. Implement rate limiting to quickly restrict the number of failed login attempts from the same IP or user account, mitigating brute-force attacks.
2. Use account lockout policies that temporarily or permanently lock accounts after a certain number of failed login attempts.

4. Multi-Factor Authentication (MFA): Combine passwords with another form of authenticati
on (like a mobile device or biometric verification) to enhance security. The attacker cannot gain access without the second factor, even if the password is compromised.

5. Password Managers: Encourage users to use password managers to generate and store strong, unique passwords for each service. This reduces the risk of password reuse across different platforms, which is a common vulnerability.

6. Preventing Phishing Attacks:

1. Educate users on recognising phishing attacks and use email filtering and phishing detection techniques.
2. Deploy two-factor authentication (2FA) to minimise the effectiveness of stolen credentials obtained through phishing.

8.4 Securing Web Authentication Mechanisms

Securing web authentication mechanisms is essential for protecting web applications from unauthorised access, identity theft, and session hijacking. Effective security measures focus on hardening the authentication process, safeguarding credentials, and mitigating common vulnerabilities.

Key Strategies for Securing Web Authentication Mechanisms:

1. Use of Secure Protocols (TLS/SSL):
    a. Transport Layer Security (TLS) should be used to encrypt all Data exchanges during the authentication process. This ensures that attackers cannot intercept or alter sensitive information, such as credentials, during transmission.
    b. Redirect HTTP traffic to HTTPS to enforce secure connections.
2. Enforce Strong Password Policies:
    a. Ensure passwords meet complexity requirements (length, use of alphanumeric and special characters) to prevent easily guessable or weak passwords.
    b. Use password strength meters to encourage users to create more secure passwords.
3. Multi-Factor Authentication (MFA):
    a. Implement MFA to add an extra layer of security. In addition to passwords, use SMS, email codes, authentication apps, or biometrics to verify the user's identity.
    b. MFA significantly reduces the risk of compromised accounts through password theft or brute-force attacks.
4. Session Management Security:

a. Use secure session cookies by setting attributes like Http Only, Secure, and Same Site. This prevents cookies from being accessed by malicious scripts, ensures they are only transmitted over secure channels, and reduces the risk of cross-site request forgery (CSRF) attacks.

b. Implement session timeout and automatic logout features to limit the duration of inactive sessions, reducing the risk of session hijacking.

5. Protect Against Brute Force and Credential Stuffing:

a. Implement rate limiting and account lockouts after a certain number of failed login attempts to mitigate brute-force attacks.

b. Use CAPTCHA or reCAPTCHA to distinguish between human users and automated bots during the login process.

6. Hashing and Salting Credentials:

a. Store passwords securely using cryptographic hashing algorithms (e.g., bcrypt, PBKDF2, Argon2).

b. Use salting to ensure that even if two users have the same password, their hashed values will differ, making it harder for attackers to use precomputed hash tables.

7. OAuth and OpenID Connect for Authentication:

a. For third-party or federated authentication, use secure protocols like OAuth 2.0 or OpenID Connect to manage tokens and sessions securely.

b. Ensure proper token validation, expiration, and revocation mechanisms are in place.

8.5 Types of Permissions in Web Applications

Permissions in web applications determine what actions users can perform and what resources they can access based on their role or identity. Properly defining and managing permissions is essential for ensuring that users only have access to the Data and functionalities appropriate to their role.

Key Types of Permissions in Web Applications:

1. Read Permissions:

Allow users to view or access Data within the application but not modify it. Common in situations where users need to reference Data without making changes.

Example: A customer can view their account balance but cannot change it.

2. Write Permissions:

Enable users to modify or create Data within the application. Users with written permissions can edit, delete, or add new records to the system.

Example: An administrator who can add new users or a customer who can update their profile information.

3. Execute Permissions:

Allow users to run specific operations or commands within the application. This could include tasks like running reports, executing scripts, or performing actions that change system states.

Example: A developer might have permission to deploy code or execute Database queries.

4. Admin/Full Control Permissions:

Provide users with complete control over the application, including the ability to manage users, roles, and settings.

Example: A system administrator who can configure security settings, modify access control policies, and monitor the application.

5. Role-Based Permissions:

Permissions are assigned based on a user's role within the organisation. Roles could include admin, editor, viewer, or guest, with each role having specific sets of permissions tied to it.

Example: An editor can modify content, while a viewer can only read it.

6. Object-Level Permissions:

Define what specific objects or resources a user can interact with. This could be based on data ownership or specific attributes of the object.

Example: A user can only modify their own account details but not those of other users.

8.6 Time of Check to Time of Use (TOCTTOU) Exploits

Time of Check to Time of Use (TOCTTOU) exploits are a type of race condition vulnerability that occurs when an attacker manipulates the state of a system between the time it checks a condition (such as verifying permissions or resource availability) and the time it uses the results of that check to operate. This brief window of time allows attackers to interfere and potentially exploit the system.

Key Concepts of TOCTTOU Exploits:
1. Time of Check (TOC): The moment when a system verifies or checks a condition, such as ensuring a user has the proper permissions or that a file is accessible.
2. Time of Use (TOU): The point when the system actually uses the check results to execute an operation, like opening a file or allowing access to a resource.
3. The Exploit: An attacker exploits the time gap between TOC and TOU by changing the system's state (such as modifying a file, permissions, or resource) after the check has been performed but before the operation is completed. This allows the attacker to bypass security checks or manipulate Data.

Example of TOCTTOU Exploit:
File Access: An application checks if a user has permission to open a file. Before the file is opened (TOU), the attacker swaps the file with a malicious one. Since the check (TOC) was already passed, the malicious file is opened, potentially causing harm.
Mitigating TOCTTOU Exploits:
1. Atomic Operations: Perform the check and use operations as a single atomic unit without allowing time for any changes between them. This reduces the time window where an attacker can interfere.
2. Locking Mechanisms: Use locks to prevent any changes to the resource (file, Data, permissions) between the time of check and the time of use, ensuring consistency.
3. Rechecking Conditions:Re-verify the condition immediately before the use operation. For example, check permissions again right before accessing a file.
4. Least Privilege: Follow the principle of least privilege, granting minimal permissions necessary for each operation, limiting the potential impact of a TOCTTOU attack.

8.7 Glossary
1. Authentication: The process of verifying a user's identity before granting access to a web application. Common methods include passwords, multi-factor authentication (MFA), and token-based systems.
2. Multi-Factor Authentication (MFA): An authentication method that requires two or more verification steps, such as something you know (password), something you have (a phone), or something you are (biometrics).
3. Three-Factor Authentication (3FA): An advanced authentication method requiring three forms of verification—typically combining knowledge (password), possession (device), and inherence (biometric).
4. Password Policies: Security measures that define the requirements for creating strong passwords, such as length, character complexity, and periodic changes, to prevent easily guessable credentials.
5. Hashing: A process of converting a password into a fixed-length string of characters, which is not reversible. It helps in storing passwords securely.
6. Salting: Adding a random string to a password before hashing makes it unique and protects it from rainbow table attacks.
7. Session Management: Techniques used to manage user sessions after authentication, including secure handling of session cookies, session expiration, and preventing session hijacking.
8. Http Only Cookie: A session cookie attribute that prevents client-side scripts from accessing the cookie, thus reducing the risk of cross-site scripting (XSS) attacks.
9. Secure Cookie: A session cookie attribute ensures cookies are only transmitted over HTTPS, preventing interception during transmission.
10. Rate Limiting: A security mechanism that restricts the number of login attempts or requests to prevent brute-force attacks.
11. OAuth: An open token-based authentication standard allowing third-party applications to access a user's information without exposing their password.
12. OpenID Connect (OIDC): A protocol built on OAuth 2.0 that provides authentication (in addition to authorisation), enabling users to log in to multiple services with a single set of credentials.

8.8 Summary

1. Basics of Web Authentication: Only authorised users can access a web application. It involves methods like username/password combinations, Multi-Factor Authentication (MFA), and token-based systems. Strong authentication practices protect against unauthorised access and identity theft.
2. Two-Factor and Three-Factor Authentication: These methods enhance security by requiring additional verification steps. Two-Factor Authentication (2FA) combines something the user knows with something the user has, while Three-Factor Authentication (3FA) adds a third factor, such as biometrics, for even greater security.
3. Securing Password-Based Authentication: Effective security measures include enforcing strong password policies, hashing and salting passwords, implementing rate limiting and account lockout mechanisms, using Multi-Factor Authentication (MFA), and educating users on phishing threats. These practices help prevent common vulnerabilities associated with password-based systems.
4. Securing Web Authentication Mechanisms: This involves using secure protocols (TLS/SSL), implementing robust session management, defending against brute-force and credential stuffing attacks, and utilising OAuth or Single Sign-On (SSO) for third-party authentication. These measures ensure the integrity and confidentiality of the authentication process.
5. Types of Permissions in Web Applications: Permissions define what users can access and modify within a web application. Types include read, write, execute, and admin permissions and more granular controls like object-level and field-level permissions. Proper permission management prevents unauthorised access and Data breaches.
6. Time of Check to Time of Use (TOCTTOU) Exploits: TOCTTOU exploits occur when an attacker manipulates the state of a system between the time it checks a condition and the time it uses the results. Mitigations include using atomic operations, implementing locking mechanisms, and rechecking conditions immediately before use.

8.9 Previous Year Solved Questions

Ques 1. How can web applications ensure secure authentication and session management, and what measures should be taken to mitigate common vulnerabilities associated with these processes? (Udaipur University, 2022 MCA)
Ans 1. Ensuring secure authentication and session management is critical for protecting web applications from unauthorised access and potential security breaches. Here's a comprehensive approach to securing these aspects, along with measures to mitigate common vulnerabilities:

1. Implement Robust Authentication Mechanisms:

- Username and Password: While traditional, passwords should be enforced with strong policies, requiring complexity and length to prevent weak credentials. Passwords should be hashed using cryptographic algorithms (e.g., bcrypt, Argon2) and salted to protect against rainbow table attacks.
- Multi-Factor Authentication (MFA): Enhances security by requiring additional verification steps. 2FA combines something the user knows (password) with something they have (a mobile device), while 3FA adds a biometric factor. This multi-layered approach significantly reduces the risk of unauthorised access even if passwords are compromised.
- Token-Based Authentication: This method utilises tokens (such as JSON Web Tokens, JWTs) issued upon successful login. These tokens should be securely stored (e.g., in HTTP-only cookies) and managed to prevent session hijacking.

2. Secure Session Management:

- Session Cookies: Use secure attributes for session cookies, including Http Only (to prevent client-side access), Secure (to ensure transmission over HTTPS), and Same Site (to protect against CSRF attacks). Implement session expiration and automatic logout features to reduce the risk of session hijacking.
- Session Tokens: Regularly regenerate session tokens to prevent session fixation attacks, especially after privilege changes or sensitive actions. Validate tokens on each request to ensure they are still valid and have not been tampered with.

3. Prevent Brute-Force and Credential Stuffing Attacks:

- Rate Limiting and Account Lockout: Implement rate limiting to restrict the number of login attempts from a single IP address or user account. Use account lockout policies to temporarily or permanently disable accounts after a certain number of failed attempts.
- CAPTCHA: Deploy CAPTCHA mechanisms to distinguish between human users and automated bots during login attempts, adding a layer of defence against brute-force attacks.

4. Utilize Secure Protocols and Practices:

- Encryption (TLS/SSL): Ensure all Data transmitted between the client and server is encrypted using TLS/SSL. This protects against man-in-the-middle attacks and eavesdropping on sensitive information, including credentials and session tokens.
- OAuth and OpenID Connect: For third-party or federated authentication, use secure protocols like OAuth 2.0 and OpenID Connect to manage tokens and sessions. Ensure proper token validation, expiration, and revocation processes are in place.

5. Manage Permissions Effectively:
• Role-Based Access Control (RBAC): Define user roles (admin, editor, viewer) with specific permissions and access rights. Ensure that users only have access to the resources and actions necessary for their roles.
• Object-Level and Field-Level Permissions: Implement granular access controls to manage what users can view or modify within specific objects or fields. This prevents unauthorised access to sensitive Data.
6. Address Time of Check to Time of Use (TOCTTOU) Vulnerabilities:
• Atomic Operations: Where possible, perform checks and subsequent actions as a single atomic operation to minimize the time window during which an attacker can exploit race conditions.
• Locking Mechanisms: Use locks or other synchronization mechanisms to prevent changes to resources between check and use.
• Rechecking Conditions: Re-validate critical conditions immediately before performing sensitive operations to ensure no unauthorised changes have occurred since the initial check.
7. Educate Users and Monitor Activity:
• User Education: Provide training and resources to help users recognise phishing attempts and other security threats.
• Logging and Monitoring: Implement comprehensive logging and monitoring for authentication and session management activities. Set up alerts for unusual patterns or suspicious behaviour, such as repeated failed login attempts or access from unknown locations.

Exercises

Exercise 1 – Multiple Choice Questions
1. What does Multi-Factor Authentication (MFA) require?
a. A single verification step
b. Two or more verification steps
c. A password only
d. A username and password

2. Which of the following helps protect against credential stuffing attacks?
a. Hashing
b. Rate Limiting
c. Field-Level Permissions
d. TOCTTOU Exploit

Exercise 2 – True/False
1. Salting adds a random string to a password before hashing to protect against rainbow table attacks.
2. OAuth is used for enhancing password strength by adding additional complexity.

Exercise 3 – Fill in the blanks
1. ________ involves converting a password into a fixed-length string of characters.
2. The process of verifying a user's identity before granting access to a web application is known as ________.

Exercise 4- Fill in the blanks with two options
1. ________ (Password Policies/Hashing) helps in storing passwords securely.
2. A ________ (Secure Cookie/Http Only Cookie) ensures cookies are only transmitted over HTTPS.

Exercise 5- Rearrange the sentence
1. Rate Limiting/number/requests/restricts/the/of/login/attempts.
2. Session Management/handling/secure/cookies/involves/techniques.

Exercise 6- Choose the Odd One Out
1. a. Multi-Factor Authentication
b. Brute Force Attack
c. Three-Factor Authentication
d. Password Policies
2. a. OAuth

b. Secure Cookie
c. Hashing
d. Role-Based Access Control

Exercise 7- Jumble words
1. OTFIRNSHA – ________
2. OIAFTEPRTNSI – ________

Exercise 8- Match case
1. Multi-Factor Authentication
2. Token-Based Authentication
3. Http Only Cookie
4. OAuth

An authentication method requiring two or more verification steps.
An open standard for token-based authentication allowing third-party access.
A session cookie attribute preventing client-side script access.
A method that combines something the user knows with something the user has.

Exercise 9- Assertion – Reason
1. Assertion: Multi-Factor Authentication (MFA) provides additional security by requiring multiple forms of verification.
Reason: MFA can involve something you know, something you have, or something you are.
a) Both Assertion and Reason are correct and Reason is the correct explanation for Assertion.
b) Both Assertion and Reason are correct but Reason is not the correct explanation for Assertion.
c) Assertion is correct but Reason is incorrect.
d) Assertion is incorrect but Reason is correct.

2. Assertion: Password Policies only involve enforcing minimum password lengths.
Reason: Password Policies may include complexity requirements and periodic changes as well.
a) Both Assertion and Reason are correct and Reason is the correct explanation for Assertion.
b) Both Assertion and Reason are correct but Reason is not the correct explanation for Assertion.
c) Assertion is correct but Reason is incorrect.
d) Assertion is incorrect but Reason is correct.

Exercise 10- Read the questions below and find the appropriate word in the provided grid.
Questions:
1. The process of verifying user identity using methods like username/password, MFA, and token-based systems is known as __________.
2. The vulnerability that arises when an attacker manipulates a system between the time it checks a condition and the time it uses the results is referred to as __________.

Grid:

M	H	O	A	I	J	B	J	Q	N	L	H	W	T	V
W	E	B	A	U	T	H	E	N	T	I	T	I	O	N
M	K	E	P	O	P	V	N	M	P	Y	H	E	C	D
D	A	I	S	N	E	S	S	N	O	U	R	E	T	E
A	R	P	S	P	O	O	F	I	N	K	W	R	T	B
T	M	N	O	S	A	F	L	H	K	L	V	A	O	A
T	Q	W	O	T	R	C	A	G	W	M	G	E	U	R
W	E	Q	R	T	Y	U	I	O	P	L	M	Z	E	Q
A	Z	X	C	V	B	N	M	D	S	F	G	H	X	Q
Q	W	Q	C	F	V	S	E	A	R	R	W	E	P	G
D	F	G	H	J	K	L	M	N	B	V	C	X	L	B
Z	X	C	V	B	N	M	L	J	H	G	G	F	O	N
V	G	Y	R	T	E	F	H	J	G	J	F	S	I	M
R	E	G	R	E	S	S	I	O	N	T	E	S	T	I

Exercise 11- One- word

1. What process involves adding a random string to a password before hashing?
2. What term describes a protocol for token-based authentication?

Exercise 12- Small Answers

1. Describe the role of Secure Cookies in web authentication.
2. What is the main purpose of Rate Limiting?

Exercise 13- Long Answers

1. Explain the importance of Multi-Factor Authentication (MFA) in enhancing web application security and list its typical components.
2. Discuss the potential vulnerabilities associated with password-based authentication and describe the best practices to mitigate these risks.

Exercise 14- Previous Year Unsolved Questions

1. Describe the advantages and disadvantages of using Three-Factor Authentication (3FA) compared to Multi-Factor Authentication (MFA) in web applications. (Delhi University, December, 2023, MCA)
2. How does the use of Http Only and Secure Cookies enhance the security of web session management? (Delhi University, December, 2023, MCA)
3. Explain the classification of cybercrimes with examples (Mumbai University, January, 2023, MCA)
4. Explain Phishing and Identity theft in details. (Mumbai University, January, 2023, MCA)
5. (a) What are the advantages and disadvantages of symmetric-key cryptography?
(b) Explain the following security measures:
    i. E-mail security
    ii. Anti-virus protection
    iii. Access security (IGNOU, January, 2023, MCA)
6. (a) What are the needs of regulating the cyberspace? Explain.
(b) Explain the role of filtering devices and rating systems in the context of legal and self regulatory framework of cyberspace. (IGNOU, January, 2023, MCA)
7. Explain the following terms in the context of cyber crimes and cyber laws and JPR issues:
    i. Cyber Forensics
    ii. Classification of cyber crimes
    iii. Domain name disputes
    iv. Framin

Answers

Exercise 1- 1. a. Password Policies, 2. b. Prevent brute-force attacks

Exercise 2- 1. True, 2. True
Exercise 3- 1. Multi-Factor Authentication (MFA), 2. Hashing
Exercise 4- 1. Dynamic/Static, 2. Software-based/Hardware-based
Exercise 5- 1. System call logging is used to track system calls., 2. Interactive sandboxes allow manual control for malware analysis.
Exercise 6- 1. d. Process Monitor, 2. System Call Logging
Exercise 7- 1. AUTHENTICATION, 2. OAUTH
Exercise 8- 1- c , 2-b , 3-a , 4-d
Exercise 9- 1. Assertion: Network simulation is crucial in malware analysis. Reason: It allows analysts to observe how malware interacts with external servers., 2. Assertion: Static analysis can uncover dynamic malware behaviors. Reason: Static analysis only examines the code without execution.
Exercise 10- 1. WEB AUTHENTICATION, 2. TOCTTOU EXPLOIT

M	H	O	A	I	J	B	J	Q	N	L	H	W	T	V
W	E	B	A	U	T	H	E	N	T	I	T	I	O	N
M	K	E	P	O	P	V	N	M	P	Y	H	E	C	D
D	A	I	S	N	E	S	S	N	O	U	R	E	T	E
A	R	P	S	P	O	O	F	I	N	K	W	R	T	B
T	M	N	O	S	A	F	L	H	K	L	V	A	O	A
T	Q	W	O	T	R	C	A	G	W	M	G	E	U	R
W	E	Q	R	T	Y	U	I	O	P	L	M	Z	E	Q
A	Z	X	C	V	B	N	M	D	S	F	G	H	X	Q
Q	W	Q	C	F	V	S	E	A	R	R	W	E	P	G
D	F	G	H	J	K	L	M	N	B	V	C	X	L	B
Z	X	C	V	B	N	M	L	J	H	G	G	F	O	N
V	G	Y	R	T	E	F	H	J	G	J	F	S	I	M
R	E	G	R	E	S	S	I	O	N	T	E	S	T	I

Exercise 11- 1. Isolation, 2. EnCase

Test Paper

Chapter-8

Web Authentication and Session Management

Time Duration: 30 Minutes **Maximum Marks: 25**

General Instructions:

1. The question paper consists of 12 questions and is divided into four sections, A, B, C and D.
2. All questions are compulsory.
3. Section A comprises MCQs, Fill in the blanks and True or False carrying one marks each.
4. Section B comprises VSAQs(very short answers questions) carrying two marks each.
5. Section C comprises SAQs(short questions) carrying four marks each.
6. Section D comprises long questions carrying five marks each.

SECTION-A

I. Multiple choice questions: **(1*2=2)**

1. Which authentication method requires three forms of verification?
a) Multi-Factor Authentication (MFA)
b) Two-Factor Authentication (2FA)
c) Single Sign-On (SSO)
d) Three-Factor Authentication (3FA)

2. What is the purpose of a Secure Cookie?
a) To prevent unauthorized access to the cookie
b) To ensure cookies are only transmitted over HTTPS
c) To make cookies accessible to JavaScript
d) To reduce the cookie's size

II. Fill in the blanks: **(1*2=2)**

1. __________ involves converting a password into a fixed-length string that cannot be reversed.
2. A security measure that adds a random string to a password before hashing is called __________.

III. True or False: **(1*2=2)**

1. Multi-Factor Authentication (MFA) combines something you know, something you have, and something you are.
2. Brute Force Attacks involve trying all possible password combinations until the correct one is found.

SECTION-B

IV. Very Short answers type questions-I **(2*3=6)**

1. Name one benefit of implementing Multi-Factor Authentication (MFA) in web applications.
2. What is the primary function of rate limiting in web authentication systems?
3. Define hashing in the context of web authentication.

SECTION-C

V. Short answers type questions-II **(4*2=8)**

1. Explain the concept of "Least Privilege" and its importance in web application security.
2. Describe the role of Http Only Cookies in enhancing the security of web sessions.

SECTION-D

VI. Long answers type questions **(5*1=5)**

1. Discuss the differences between Two-Factor Authentication (2FA) and Three-Factor Authentication (3FA), highlighting their respective advantages and potential drawbacks in web authentication systems.

ONLINE RESOURCES

Practice Paper
Link: https://forms.gle/YEGcqcSqLKP7ZP9m8
QR Code:

YouTube Video Playlist Link
Link: https://www.youtube.com/playlist?list=PLzlh_31VWEFphqGbLIapdVFOs1oxnmIAs
QR Code:

Chapter 9 - Legal and Ethical Issues in Cyber Security

In this chapter you will learn about:
Introduction to Cyber Law
Essential Principles of Criminal Law
Mens Rea and Actus Reus in Cyber Crimes
Offences and Penalties under the IT Act 2000
Cyber Stalking and Cyber Terrorism
Digital Forgery and Obscenity Laws
Cyber Pornography Regulations
Legal Framework for Hacking and Fraud
Corporate Responsibility in Cyber Security
Ethical Issues in Cybersecurity

Legal and Ethical Issues in Cyber Security explore the framework within which cyber security professionals operate, focusing on the legal obligations and ethical principles that guide their actions. As technology advances and cyber threats become more sophisticated, understanding these issues is crucial for ensuring compliance, protecting privacy, and maintaining the integrity of cyber security practices.

9.1 Essential Principles of Criminal Law

Essential Principles of Criminal Law form the foundation of how criminal behaviour is defined, prosecuted, and adjudicated. These principles ensure that legal proceedings are fair, just, and effective in addressing criminal activities. Understanding these principles is crucial for those involved in cyber security, as they often intersect with legal frameworks for addressing cyber crimes.

Key Principles:

1. Legality (Nullum Crimen, Nulla Poena Sine Lege):

Definition: A fundamental principle stating that no one can be prosecuted or punished for an act unless it is defined as a crime by law before the act was committed. This ensures that individuals are not punished retroactively.

Application: In cyber security, this means that actions taken by individuals or organizations must be clearly defined as illegal in current laws before they can be prosecuted.

2. Actus Reus (The Criminal Act):

Definition: Refers to the physical act or conduct that constitutes a criminal offense. It is the actual behavior that breaches the law.

Application: For cyber crimes, actus reus includes unauthorized access to systems, Data breaches, and other illegal activities performed using technology.

3. Mens Rea (The Mental State):

Definition: The mental state or intent of the person committing the crime. It refers to the criminal intent or knowledge that an individual had at the time of committing the act.

Application: In cyber crimes, mens rea involves understanding whether the perpetrator intended to commit the offense or acted with recklessness or negligence.

4. Concurrence:

Definition: The principle that the actus reus and mens rea must occur simultaneously. Both the criminal act and the intent must be present at the same time for a crime to be established.

Application: For a cyber crime to be prosecuted, there must be evidence that the act was performed with the requisite criminal intent or knowledge.

5. Causation:

Definition: Establishes a link between the defendant's actions and the harm or damage caused. It ensures that the defendant's conduct is the direct cause of the criminal outcome.

Application: In cyber security, this means proving that a hacker's actions directly caused the Data breach or damage to the system.

6. Harm:

Definition: Refers to the injury or damage caused by the criminal act. It can be physical, financial, or reputational harm.

Application: Cyber crimes often result in financial loss, Data breaches, or disruption of services, and proving harm is crucial for establishing the severity of the crime.

7. Defence and Justification:

Definition: Legal defenses that can negate or reduce criminal liability. Common defenses include self-defense, duress, or lack of intent.

Application: In cyber crime cases, defenses might include claims that actions were taken under duress or without criminal intent.

9.2 Mens Rea and Actus Reus in Cyber Crimes

Understanding mens rea (the mental state) and actus reus (the criminal act) is crucial for defining criminal liability and pursuing justice in cyber crimes. These concepts help establish the elements required to prosecute cyber criminals effectively.

Actus Reus (The Criminal Act)

Actus reus refers to the actual conduct or action that constitutes a criminal offence. In cyber crimes, actus reus includes:

Unauthorized Access: Gaining entry into a computer system, network, or Database without permission. This could involve bypassing security measures or exploiting vulnerabilities.

Data Breach: Illegally obtaining or exposing sensitive or Personal data, such as financial information, personal identification details, or confidential business Data.

Malware Distribution: Creating, spreading, or deploying malicious software (malware) to damage, disrupt, or gain unauthorised access to systems.

Denial of Service (DoS) Attacks involve overloading a network or server to disrupt its normal functioning and deny access to legitimate users.

Phishing Is fraudulent activity in which someone pretends to be trustworthy to deceive individuals into revealing sensitive information, such as login credentials or financial details.

Data Manipulation: Altering or destroying Data without authorisation leads to corruption or information loss.

Mens Rea (The Mental State)

Mens rea refers to the mental state or intent of the person committing the crime. It involves the perpetrator's state of mind at the time of the offense and can include:

Intent: The deliberate and conscious decision to commit a crime. For cyber crimes, the perpetrator knowingly performed actions such as hacking or distributing malware to cause harm or obtain unauthorised benefits.

Knowledge: Awareness that one's actions will likely result in criminal conduct. For example, knowing that accessing a restricted network or Database without permission is illegal.

Recklessness: Disregarding the substantial risk that one's actions could cause harm. In cyber crimes, this may involve actions taken with a wilful disregard for the potential consequences, such as spreading malware without concern for its impact.

Negligence: Failing to be aware of a risk that a reasonable person would recognise. In cyber contexts, negligence might involve poor security practices that lead to a Data breach, where the perpetrator did not intentionally cause harm but acted with a lack of due care.

Applying Mens Rea and Actus Reus to Cyber Crimes

Establishing Actus Reus: Prosecutors must prove that the defendant engaged in specific criminal actions related to cyber crimes, such as unauthorised Data access or malware deployment. This involves demonstrating that the actions fit the legal definition of the crime.

Establishing Mens Rea: The prosecution must also show that the defendant had the necessary mental state at the time of the offence. This might include evidence of intent to commit the crime, knowledge of its illegal nature, or recklessness in carrying out the actions.

Defences: Defendants might argue that they lacked the requisite mens rea, such as claiming they did not intend to commit a crime or were unaware that their actions were illegal. Alternatively, they might argue that the actus reus was not present, such as claiming they did not access restricted systems.

9.3 Offences and Penalties under the IT Act 2000

The Information Technology Act 2000 (IT Act 2000) is a key legislation in India that addresses various aspects of cybercrime and electronic commerce. It defines specific offences and associated penalties related to the misuse of technology and Data. Here's an overview of the significant offences and penalties under this Act:

1. Hacking and Unauthorized Access
Section 66: Deals with hacking and unauthorised access to computer systems.
- **Offence**: Hacking into computer systems or Data, including gaining unauthorised access or damaging Data.
- **Penalty**: Imprisonment for up to three years, a fine up to five lakh rupees, or both.

2. Identity Theft and Data Theft
Section 66C: Addresses identity theft.
- **Offence**: Using someone else's identity information without authorisation for fraudulent activities.
- **Penalty**: Imprisonment for up to three years, a fine up to one lakh rupees, or both.

Section 66D: Deals with cheating by impersonation using computer resources.
- **Offence**: Using false identity or impersonating others through technology to deceive or cheat.
- **Penalty**: Imprisonment for up to three years, a fine up to one lakh rupees, or both.

3. Cyber Terrorism
Section 66F: Addresses cyber terrorism.
- **Offence**: Engaging in activities that threaten India's integrity, security, or sovereignty through cyber means.
- **Penalty**: Imprisonment for a term that may extend to life imprisonment and a fine as decided by the court.

4. Obscenity and Pornography
Section 67: Relates to the transmission of obscene material in electronic form.
- **Offence**: Publishing or transmitting obscene material through electronic means.
- **Penalty**: Imprisonment for up to five years and a fine of up to ten lakh rupees. For repeat offenders, imprisonment can extend up to seven years, and the fine can increase.

Section 67A: Deals with the transmission of material containing sexually explicit content.
- **Offence**: Disseminating sexually explicit content electronically.
- **Penalty**: Imprisonment for up to five years and a fine of up to ten lakh rupees, which can be extended for repeat offenders.

5. Cyber Stalking and Harassment
Section 66E: Addresses violation of privacy.
- **Offence**: Capturing, publishing, or transmitting images of a person without their consent, including acts of cyberstalking or harassment.
- **Penalty**: Imprisonment for up to three years, a fine up to two lakh rupees, or both.

9.4 Cyber Stalking and Cyber Terrorism

Cyber Stalking and **Cyber Terrorism** are serious offences under cyber law, targeting individuals and institutions through digital means. Understanding these crimes and their legal implications is crucial for prevention and prosecution.

Cyber Stalking

Definition:

Cyber Stalking involves using electronic communications to harass or intimidate an individual. It includes repeated, unwanted, and intrusive messages or actions that cause distress or fear.

Legal Framework under IT Act 2000:

Section 66E: Addresses the violation of privacy through capturing, publishing, or transmitting images or personal information without consent.
- **Offence**: Capturing and sharing private images or information without the individual's consent, often used in cyberstalking cases.
- **Penalty**: Imprisonment for up to three years, a fine up to two lakh rupees, or both.

Additional Measures:

Section 354D (Indian Penal Code, IPC): Specifically targets stalking, including cyberstalking.
- **Offence**: Engaging in persistent, unwanted communication or behaviour that causes fear or distress.
- **Penalty**: Imprisonment for up to three years, with a possible fine.

Cyber Terrorism

Definition:

Cyber Terrorism refers to using cyber capabilities to threaten or disrupt national security, infrastructure, or public safety. It involves activities intended to cause severe harm or panic through digital means.

Legal Framework under IT Act 2000:

Section 66F: Specifically addresses cyber terrorism.
- **Offence**: Engaging in activities that threaten India's security, integrity, or sovereignty through cyber means.

Penalty: Imprisonment for a term that may extend to life imprisonment, with fines as determined by the court.

Additional Considerations:

Terrorism Laws: Cyberterrorism may also be prosecuted under anti-terrorism laws and regulations that deal with acts threatening national security.

Preventive and Mitigative Measures

1. For Cyber Stalking:

Legal Actions: Victims should report incidents to law enforcement and seek protection under relevant sections of the IPC and IT Act.

Support Services: Utilize support services such as counselling and legal aid for cyberstalking victims.

2. For Cyber Terrorism:

Security Measures: Organizations and governments should implement robust cyber security measures to protect critical infrastructure.

Collaboration: Cooperation between national and international agencies is essential for effectively combating and responding to cyberterrorism threats.

9.5 Digital Forgery and Obscenity Laws

Digital Forgery and **Obscenity** are significant issues within cyber law, addressing fraudulent activities and distributing inappropriate content in the digital realm. Here's a breakdown of these issues under the IT Act 2000 and other relevant laws:

Digital Forgery

Definition:

Digital Forgery involves altering, manipulating, or creating digital documents or records with fraudulent intent. It often includes forging electronic signatures or tampering with digital evidence.

Legal Framework under IT Act 2000:

Section 66D: Addresses cheating by impersonation using computer resources.

Offence: Using forged electronic documents or identities to deceive others.

Penalty: Imprisonment for up to three years, a fine up to one lakh rupees, or both.

Section 65: Deals with tampering with computer source documents.

Offence: Altering or falsifying computer source codes or documents intending to deceive or commit fraud.

Penalty: Imprisonment for up to three years, a fine up to two lakh rupees, or both.

Obscenity Laws

Definition:

Obscenity refers to the distribution or display of material that is sexually explicit, indecent, or offensive. In the digital context, this includes online pornography and other inappropriate content.

Legal Framework under IT Act 2000:

Section 67: Addresses the publication and transmission of obscene material in electronic form.

Offence: Publishing, transmitting, or causing to be published obscene material through electronic means.

Penalty: Up to five years in prison and a fine of up to ten lakh rupees. For repeat offenders, imprisonment can extend to seven years, and the fine can be increased.

Section 67A: Deals with sexually explicit content.

Offence: Disseminating sexually explicit content through electronic means.

Penalty: Imprisonment for up to five years and a fine of up to ten lakh rupees, with enhanced penalties for repeat offenders.

9.6 Cyber Pornography Regulations

Cyber Pornography refers to the distribution, access, or viewing of sexually explicit material over digital platforms. The regulation of cyber pornography is crucial to prevent abuse, protect minors, and uphold community standards. Here's an overview of the regulatory framework and measures in place under Indian law:

Legal Framework

1. Information Technology Act, 2000 (IT Act 2000)

Section 67: Addresses the publication and transmission of obscene material in electronic form.

Offence: Publishing, transmitting, or causing to be published any obscene material electronically.

Penalty: Imprisonment for up to five years and a fine of up to ten lakh rupees. Repeat offenders may face imprisonment of up to seven years and increased fines.

Section 67A: Specifically deals with sexually explicit content.

Offence: Disseminating or transmitting sexually explicit content through electronic means.

Penalty: Imprisonment for up to five years and a fine of up to ten lakh rupees. Repeat offenders may face extended imprisonment and higher fines.

Section 67B: Focuses on content involving minors.

Offence: Publishing, transmitting, or causing to be published any material involving children in sexually explicit acts.

Penalty: Imprisonment for up to five years and a fine of up to ten lakh rupees. Repeat offenders may face more severe penalties.

2. Indian Penal Code (IPC)

Section 292: Deals with the sale, distribution, or public exhibition of obscene material.

Offence: Disseminating obscene material in any form, including digital platforms.

Penalty: Imprisonment for up to two years and a fine, or both.

Section 293: Addresses the sale or distribution of obscene materials to minors.

Offence: Selling or distributing obscene material to individuals under 18 years of age.

Penalty: Imprisonment for up to five years and a fine.

Regulatory and Enforcement Measures

1. Content Monitoring and Filtering

Internet Service Providers (ISPs): ISPs must implement measures to block access to websites and content deemed obscene or illegal under Indian law.

Content Moderation: Platforms and social media companies must actively monitor and filter obscene content to comply with legal standards.

2. Reporting Mechanisms

Complaint Filing: Individuals can report instances of cyber pornography to law enforcement agencies or through online grievance redressal systems provided by the government.

Cyber Crime Cells: Specialized units within law enforcement agencies focus on investigating and prosecuting cases related to cyber pornography.

3. International Cooperation

Cross-border Coordination: India collaborates with international agencies to tackle cyber pornography that transcends national boundaries, ensuring that offenders are pursued and prosecuted effectively.

4. Educational and Awareness Campaigns

Public Awareness: Initiatives to educate the public about the risks and legal implications of cyber pornography, including the potential harm to minors and legal consequences for offenders.

9.7 Legal Framework for Hacking and Fraud

Hacking and **fraud** are significant concerns in the digital realm, involving unauthorised access and deceitful activities through technology. The legal framework addressing these issues in India includes various laws and regulations designed to combat and penalise such offences.

Hacking

Definition:

Hacking involves unauthorised access to computer systems, networks, or Data, often leading to Data theft, damage, or disruption.

Legal Framework under IT Act 2000:

1. Section 66: Pertains to hacking.

Offence: Unauthorized access to computer systems or Data, including manipulating or altering Data without permission.

Penalty: Imprisonment for up to three years, a fine up to five lakh rupees, or both.

2. Section 65: Deals with tampering with computer source documents.

Offence: Altering, destroying, or concealing computer source codes or documents with intent to deceive or commit fraud.

Penalty: Imprisonment for up to three years, a fine up to two lakh rupees, or both.

Additional Laws:

Indian Penal Code (IPC)

Section 378: Addresses theft, including digital theft.

Offence: Theft of Data or digital assets.

Penalty: Imprisonment or fine, based on the specifics of the crime.

Section 420: Covers cheating and dishonestly inducing delivery of property.

Offence: Committing fraud or deceit that results in property loss or damage.

Penalty: Imprisonment for up to seven years and a fine.

Fraud

Definition:

Fraud involves deceitful practices intended to unlawfully secure financial or personal gain, including through digital means such as phishing or identity theft.

Legal Framework under IT Act 2000:

Section 66D: Addresses cheating by impersonation using computer resources.

Offence: Using forged or stolen identities to deceive or commit fraud via digital platforms.

Penalty: Imprisonment for up to three years, a fine up to one lakh rupees, or both.

Section 66C: Deals with identity theft.

Offence: Using someone else's identification details without authorisation.

Penalty: Imprisonment for up to three years, a fine up to one lakh rupees, or both.

Additional Laws:

Indian Penal Code (IPC)

Section 463: Addresses forgery, including digital forgery.

Offence: Falsifying electronic documents or signatures.

Penalty: Imprisonment or fine, depending on the severity of the forgery.

Section 471: Deals with using forged documents as genuine.

Offence: Using forged documents with fraudulent intent.

Penalty: Imprisonment or fine, based on the context of the offence.

9.8 Glossary

1. Hacking: Unauthorized access to or manipulation of computer systems, networks, or Data. It often involves breaking into systems to steal, alter, or damage information.
2. Fraud: Deceptive practices intended to secure financial or personal gain unlawfully. Includes activities such as phishing, identity theft, and digital forgery.
3. Cyber Stalking: Repeated, unwanted, and intrusive online behaviour aimed at harassing or intimidating an individual, often through electronic communications.
4. Cyber Terrorism: Use of cyber capabilities to threaten or disrupt national security, infrastructure, or public safety. Involves activities intended to cause severe harm or panic through digital means.
5. Digital Forgery: Alteration or creating digital documents or records with fraudulent intent, including using forged electronic signatures or tampered digital evidence.
6. Obscenity: Distribution or display of sexually explicit, indecent, or offensive material, primarily through digital platforms. Regulated to prevent harm and maintain community standards.
7. Cyber Pornography: Distribution, access, or viewing of sexually explicit material over digital platforms. Regulated to protect individuals, especially minors, and to uphold legal standards.
8. Identity Theft: Unauthorized use of someone else's personal information for fraudulent activities, including accessing accounts or committing fraud using stolen identities.
9. Tampering with Computer Source Documents: Altering or destroying computer source codes or documents with intent to deceive or commit fraud.
10. Section 66: The IT Act 2000 provision addresses hacking, unauthorised access, and Data manipulation. Penalties include imprisonment and fines.
11. Section 66C: A provision under the IT Act 2000 related to identity theft, with penalties including imprisonment and fines.
12. Section 66D: A provision under the IT Act 2000 addressing cheating by impersonation using computer resources.
13. Section 67: The IT Act 2000 provision addresses the electronic publication and transmission of obscene material.
14. Section 67A: A provision under the IT Act 2000 focusing on sexually explicit content.
15. Section 67B: A provision under the IT Act 2000 concerning material involving minors in sexually explicit acts.
16. Section 72: A provision under the IT Act 2000 dealing with breach of confidentiality and privacy.
17. Indian Penal Code (IPC): A comprehensive criminal code in India that includes provisions relevant to hacking, fraud, forgery, and other offences.
18. Chain of Custody: The process of maintaining and documenting the handling of evidence to ensure its integrity and authenticity throughout an investigation.

19. Cyber Crime Cells: Specialized units within law enforcement agencies focused on investigating and addressing cyber crimes, including hacking and fraud.
20. Incident Response: Procedures and actions to manage and address cyber incidents, including hacking and fraud.
21. Regulatory Measures: Legal and procedural frameworks established to control and prevent specific types of offences, including cyber-related crimes.
22. International Cooperation: Collaborative efforts between countries to address cross-border cyber crimes and ensure effective law enforcement and prosecution.

9.9 Summary

Essential Principles of Criminal Law

Overview: Establishes foundational principles of criminal law, including legality, culpability, and punishment. These principles guide the enforcement of laws related to cyber crimes.

Key Points:

Legality: No crime or punishment without a law.

Culpability: Liability for actions based on intent and knowledge.

Punishment: Proportional to the severity of the crime.

Mens Rea and Actus Reus in Cyber Crimes

Mens Rea (Mental State): Refers to the criminal intent or knowledge required to establish guilt in cyber crimes.

Actus Reus (Physical Act): Involves the actual commission of the crime, such as unauthorised access or Data manipulation.

Key Points:Both mental state and physical act must be proven for a conviction in cyber crimes.

Offences and Penalties under the IT Act 2000

Overview: Describes cyber crimes defined under the IT Act 2000, including hacking, identity theft, and cyber pornography.

Key Points:

Hacking (Section 66): Unauthorized access with penalties of up to three years' imprisonment.

Identity Theft (Section 66C): Unauthorized use of personal Data with similar penalties.

Cyber Pornography (Sections 67, 67A, 67B): Prohibits obscene and explicit content, with severe penalties for violations.

Cyber Stalking and Cyber Terrorism

Cyber Stalking: Persistent online harassment causing distress or fear.

Legal Measures: Section 66E of the IT Act and Section 354D of the IPC address cyberstalking.

Cyber Terrorism: Threats or attacks aimed at national security through digital means.

Legal Measures: Section 66F of the IT Act addresses acts of cyber terrorism with potential life imprisonment.

Digital Forgery and Obscenity Laws

Digital Forgery: Involves creating or altering digital documents fraudulently.

Legal Measures: Section 66D (cheating by impersonation) and Section 65 (tampering with source documents) of the IT Act.

Obscenity: Covers distribution of sexually explicit or offensive material.

Legal Measures: Sections 67, 67A, and 67B of the IT Act regulate obscene content, with penalties including imprisonment and fines.

Cyber Pornography Regulations

Overview: Addresses the regulation and control of sexually explicit material distributed digitally.

Key Points:

IT Act Sections 67, 67A, 67B: Prohibit publishing or transmitting obscene and explicit content.

Regulatory Measures: Involve monitoring, filtering, and reporting mechanisms to combat cyber pornography.

Legal Framework for Hacking and Fraud

Hacking: Unauthorized access or manipulation of computer systems.

Legal Measures: Section 66 (hacking) and Section 65 (tampering) of IT Act.

Fraud: Deceptive practices like phishing and digital forgery.

Legal Measures: Section 66D (cheating) and Section 66C (identity theft) of the IT Act and relevant IPC sections.

9.10 Previous Year Solved Questions

Question. Discuss the legal and ethical considerations surrounding cyber crimes, explicitly focusing on hacking, fraud, cyber pornography, and digital forgery. How does the Information Technology Act of 2000 address these issues, and what are the penalties associated with these crimes? (Mumbai University, 2022 MCA)

Answer. The legal and ethical considerations surrounding cyber crimes are multifaceted, encompassing various aspects of law, technology, and societal impact. The Information Technology Act 2000 (IT Act 2000) is a key piece of legislation in India that addresses several types of cyber crimes, including hacking, fraud, cyber pornography, and digital forgery. These crimes present unique challenges and require specific legal measures to manage and mitigate their impact.

Hacking

Legal Considerations:

- **Definition**: Hacking involves unauthorised access to or manipulation of computer systems, networks, or Data. It includes breaking into systems to steal, alter, or damage information.
- **Ethical Considerations**: Hacking raises ethical issues related to privacy, Data integrity, and the unauthorised use of digital resources.

Legal Framework under IT Act 2000:

- **Section 66**: Addresses the act of hacking by making unauthorised access a punishable offence.
- **Penalty**: Imprisonment for up to three years, a fine up to five lakh rupees, or both.
- **Section 65**: Deals tampering with computer source documents, often accompanying hacking activities.
- **Penalty**: Imprisonment for up to three years, a fine up to two lakh rupees, or both.

Fraud

Legal Considerations:

- **Definition**: Fraud involves deceitful practices intended to secure unlawful gains. This includes phishing, identity theft, and digital forgery.
- **Ethical Considerations**: Fraud undermines trust in digital systems and can lead to significant financial and personal harm.

Legal Framework under IT Act 2000:

- **Section 66D**: Addresses cheating by impersonation using computer resources.
- **Penalty**: Imprisonment for up to three years, a fine up to one lakh rupees, or both.
- **Section 66C**: This covers identity theft, where someone uses another's data without authorisation.
- **Penalty**: Imprisonment for up to three years, a fine up to one lakh rupees, or both.

Additional IPC Provisions:

- **Section 378**: Covers theft of digital assets, with penalties varying based on the specifics of the theft.
- **Section 420**: Addresses cheating and dishonestly inducing delivery of property, including through digital means.

Cyber Pornography

Legal Considerations:

- **Definition**: Cyber pornography involves the distribution and access to sexually explicit material through digital platforms.
- **Ethical Considerations**: It raises concerns about exploitation, particularly of minors, and the potential for harm caused by exposure to inappropriate content.

Legal Framework under IT Act 2000:

- **Section 67**: Prohibits the publication and transmission of obscene material electronically.
- **Penalty**: Imprisonment for up to five years and a fine of up to ten lakh rupees. Repeat offenders may face up to seven years' imprisonment and increased fines.
- **Section 67A**: Addresses sexually explicit content.
- **Penalty**: Similar penalties as Section 67.
- **Section 67B**: Focuses on material involving minors in sexually explicit acts.
- **Penalty**: Imprisonment for up to five years and a fine of up to ten lakh rupees, with enhanced penalties for repeat offenders.

Digital Forgery

Legal Considerations:

- **Definition**: Digital forgery involves altering or creating digital documents or records with fraudulent intent.
- **Ethical Considerations**: It undermines the authenticity and reliability of digital records, leading to potential misuse and legal complications.

Legal Framework under IT Act 2000:

- **Section 66D**: Also covers cheating by impersonation, which can involve digital forgery.
- **Section 65**: Deals specifically with tampering with computer source documents.
- **Penalty**: As noted, imprisonment for up to three years or a fine.

Additional IPC Provisions:

Section 463: Addresses forgery, including digital forgery.
Penalty: Imprisonment or fines depending on the severity of the forgery.
Section 471: Concerns the use of forged documents as genuine.
Penalty: Imprisonment or fines based on context.

Exercises

Exercise 1 – Multiple Choice Questions

1. Which section of the IT Act 2000 deals with identity theft?
a) Section 66
b) Section 66C
c) Section 67
d) Section 72

2. What is the legal measure for cyber terrorism under the IT Act 2000?
a) Section 66E
b) Section 67A
c) Section 66F
d) Section 72

Exercise 2 – True/False

1. Section 67B of the IT Act 2000 deals with obscenity involving minors. (True/False)
2. Cyber Stalking is regulated under the Indian Penal Code (IPC). (True/False)

Exercise 3 – Fill in the blanks

1. __________ involves the unauthorized alteration or creation of digital documents for fraudulent purposes. (Digital Forgery)
2. __________ refers to the practice of using someone else's personal information unlawfully. (Identity Theft)

Exercise 4- Fill in the blanks with two options

1. Section 66 of the IT Act 2000 deals with __________ or unauthorized access. (Hacking/Identity Theft)
2. __________ involves the publication or transmission of sexually explicit content. (Cyber Pornography/Obscenity)

Exercise 5- Rearrange the sentence

1. (Theft/identity/IT Act/Section 66C/addresses)
2. (Digital Forgery/creating/for/involves/alteration/documents)

Exercise 6- Choose the Odd One Out

1. Digital Forgery, Identity Theft, Section 67B, Cyber Stalking
2. Section 66F, Cyber Terrorism, Section 72, Hacking

Exercise 7- Jumble words

1. ETRCTEIO NHIAVYT
2. TINACELYNV DFMAPOETANL

Exercise 8- Match case

1. Section 66
2. Cyber Stalking
3. Digital Forgery
4. Section 67B

A. Identity Theft
B. Section 66E
C. Persistent Online Harassment
D. Tampering with Digital Documents

Exercise 9- Assertion – Reason

1. Assertion: Section 66F of the IT Act addresses cyber terrorism. Reason: Cyber terrorism involves threats to national security through digital means.
a) Both Assertion and Reason are correct and Reason is the correct explanation for Assertion.
b) Both Assertion and Reason are correct but Reason is not the correct explanation for Assertion.
c) Assertion is correct but Reason is incorrect.
d) Assertion is incorrect but Reason is correct.
2. Assertion: Digital Forgery is regulated under Section 66D of the IT Act. Reason: Digital Forgery includes altering or creating fraudulent documents.
a) Both Assertion and Reason are correct and Reason is the correct explanation for Assertion.
b) Both Assertion and Reason are correct but Reason is not the correct explanation for Assertion.
c) Assertion is correct but Reason is incorrect.
d) Assertion is incorrect but Reason is correct.

Exercise 10- Read the questions below and find the appropriate word in the provided grid.
Questions:

1. The principle that states no crime or punishment can exist without a law is known as __________.
2. The legal measure addressing threats or attacks aimed at national security through digital means is __________.

Grid:

Q	L	A	I	J	B	J	Q	N	L	H	W
W	E	B	T	E	R	R	O	R	I	S	M
E	G	P	O	P	V	N	M	P	Y	H	E
R	A	S	N	E	S	S	N	O	U	R	E
T	L	S	P	O	O	F	I	N	K	W	R
Y	I	O	S	A	F	L	H	K	L	V	A
U	T	O	T	R	C	A	G	W	M	G	E
I	Y	R	E	S	S	I	O	N	T	E	S

Exercise 11- One- word

1. What is the legal term for using someone else's personal information unlawfully? (Identity Theft)
2. Which section of the IT Act addresses cyber pornography? (Section 67)

Exercise 12- Small Answers

1. What is the primary penalty for hacking under the IT Act 2000?
2. Explain the term "Cyber Terrorism" in one sentence.

Exercise 13- Long Answers

1. Discuss the role of international cooperation in combating cyber crimes, including examples of international treaties and organizations involved.
2. Explain the differences between Digital Forgery and Cyber Pornography, including their legal measures under the IT Act 2000.

Exercise 14- Previous Year Unsolved Questions

1. Describe the key legal provisions under the IT Act 2000 for addressing cyber crimes and their penalties. (Udaipur University, January 2022, MCA)
2. Analyze the impact of digital forensics in investigating and prosecuting cyber crimes, with reference to chain of custody and evidence handling. (Udaipur University, January 2022, MCA)
3. How can technology be used to answer the following security issues? (IGNOU, June 2023, MCA)
   (i) Unauthorized access

(ii) Malwares
(iii) Phishing

4. What is the use of cryptography? Explain the concept of substitution cipher with the help of an example. (IGNOU, June 2023, MCA)

5. (a) Explain the concept and uses of digital signature and digital certificates. (IGNOU, June 2023, MCA)
(b) Explain the following term:
(i) Security audit
(ii) Security policy

6. (a) What is the purpose of using filtering devices and rating system on the Internet? Discuss the offences in the context of regulation of cyber law content in India.
(b) List the four categories of cyber crimes. List various cyber crimes of each category. How is cyber crime different from traditional crime? (IGNOU, June 2023, MCA)

7. (a) What is cyber forensics? Explain with the help of an example.
(b) What is Trademark? What are the different types of remedies available against infringement of trademark? (IGNOU, June 2023, MCA)

Answers

Exercise 1- 1. b) Section 66C, 2. c) Section 66F
Exercise 2- 1. True, 2. True
Exercise 3- 1. Digital Forgery, 2. Identity Theft
Exercise 4- 1. Hacking, 2. Cyber Pornography
Exercise 5- 1. Section 66C addresses identity theft., 2. Digital Forgery involves creating or altering documents for fraudulent purposes.
Exercise 6- 1. Section 67B, 2. Section 72
Exercise 7- 1. EXTRACTION IDENTITY, 2. ACTIVITY TAMPERED
Exercise 8- 1 – a, 2 – c, 3 – d, 4 – b
Exercise 9- 1. a) Both Assertion and Reason are correct and Reason is the correct explanation for Assertion., 2. a) Both Assertion and Reason are correct and Reason is the correct explanation for Assertion.
Exercise 10- 1. LEGALITY, 2. WEB TERRORISM

Q	L	A	I	J	B	J	Q	N	L	H	W
W	E	B	T	E	R	R	O	R	I	S	M
E	G	P	O	P	V	N	M	P	Y	H	E
R	A	S	N	E	S	S	N	O	U	R	E
T	L	S	P	O	O	F	I	N	K	W	R
Y	I	O	S	A	F	L	H	K	L	V	A
U	T	O	T	R	C	A	G	W	M	G	E
I	Y	R	E	S	S	I	O	N	T	E	S

Exercise 11- 1. Identity Theft, 2. Section 67

Test Paper

Chapter-9

Legal and Ethical Issues in Cyber Security

Time Duration: 30 Minutes **Maximum Marks: 25**

General Instructions:

1. The question paper consists of 12 questions and is divided into four sections, A, B, C and D.
2. All questions are compulsory.
3. Section A comprises MCQs, Fill in the blanks and True or False carrying one marks each.
4. Section B comprises VSAQs(very short answers questions) carrying two marks each.
5. Section C comprises SAQs(short questions) carrying four marks each.
6. Section D comprises long questions carrying five marks each.

SECTION-A

I. Multiple choice questions: **(1*2=2)**

1. Which section of the IT Act 2000 addresses identity theft?
a) Section 66
b) Section 66C
c) Section 67
d) Section 67B

2. Which term refers to the alteration or creation of digital documents with fraudulent intent?
a) Identity Theft
b) Digital Forgery
c) Cyber Stalking
d) Obscenity

II. Fill in the blanks: **(1*2=2)**

1. ____________ involves unauthorized access to or manipulation of computer systems and Data.
2. ____________ is a legal provision under the IT Act 2000 that addresses the publication and transmission of obscene material in electronic form.

III. True or False: **(1*2=2)**

1. Section 66F of the IT Act 2000 deals with cyber terrorism.
2. Digital Forgery includes creating or altering digital documents fraudulently.

SECTION-B

IV. Very Short answers type questions-I **(2*3=6)**

1. What is the primary purpose of Section 66C of the IT Act 2000?
2. Explain the concept of Cyber Stalking.
3. What does Chain of Custody ensure in cyber crime investigations?

SECTION-C

V. Short answers type questions-II **(4*2=8)**

1. Describe the key penalties for hacking under the IT Act 2000.
2. What are the differences between Cyber Pornography and Digital Forgery in terms of legal measures?

SECTION-D

VI. Long answers type questions **(5*1=5)**

1. Discuss the role of International Cooperation in combating cross-border cyber crimes and the challenges associated with it.

ONLINE RESOURCES

Practice Paper

Link: https://forms.gle/giPR1QQEgiUunosA7

QR Code:

YouTube Video Playlist Link

Link: https://www.youtube.com/playlist?list=PLzlh_31VWEFp4fLLNYOxy3R92HV0elpk7

QR Code:

Chapter 10 - **Law of Evidence in Cyber Crimes**

In this chapter you will learn about:
Definition of Electronic Evidence
Admissibility of Electronic Evidence
Relevance of Electronic Evidence (Sections 65A & 65B)
Proof of Electronic Signatures (Section 67A)
Verification of Digital Signatures (Section 73A)
Presumptions under Evidence Act (85A, 85B, 85C)
Handling and Preservation of Electronic Evidence
Challenges in Presenting Electronic Evidence in Court
International Perspectives on Electronic Evidence
Future Trends in Digital Evidence Law

The **Law of Evidence** in cyber crimes encompasses the rules and principles governing the collection, presentation, and evaluation of digital evidence in legal proceedings. As cyber crimes become increasingly prevalent, the importance of understanding and applying these rules effectively has grown significantly. This introduction covers the foundational aspects of digital evidence law, focusing on the unique challenges and considerations associated with cyber crimes.

10.1 Definition of Electronic Evidence

Electronic Evidence refers to any Data or information that exists in a digital format and can be used in legal proceedings. It encompasses a broad range of materials and is crucial in modern legal cases due to the prevalence of digital technology. Key components include:
Emails: Electronic communications sent and received via email systems. These can include headers, body content, attachments, and metaData that provide context for the communication.
Digital Documents: Files created, modified, or stored in digital formats such as PDFs, Word documents, spreadsheets, and presentations. These documents may contain text, images, and other Data pertinent to legal cases.
System Logs: Logs generated by operating systems, applications, and network devices that record system activities, user actions, errors, and security events. They are vital for reconstructing events and verifying system behaviour.
Multimedia Files: Digital audio, video, and image files. These files can provide visual and auditory evidence of events, interactions, or conditions relevant to a case.
Databases: Structured data collections that can include records of transactions, user activity, and other relevant information.
MetaData: Data about Data, such as file creation dates, modification histories, and access records, which can help establish the authenticity and timeline of electronic evidence.

10.2 Admissibility of Electronic Evidence

Admissibility pertains to the criteria that electronic evidence must satisfy to be accepted by the court. This includes:
Relevance: Evidence must be pertinent to the case at hand. It should contribute to proving or disproving a material fact.
Reliability: The evidence must be obtained from a trustworthy source using reliable methods. This means ensuring the evidence was collected and preserved correctly without alteration or tampering.
Authenticity: To be admitted, electronic evidence must be shown to be genuine. This involves verifying that the Data has not been altered and is what it claims to be. Authenticity can be proven through digital signatures, timestamps, and certification from credible sources.
Chain of Custody: The process of documenting every person who handles the evidence, from its collection to its presentation in court. This documentation is crucial for maintaining the evidence's integrity and proving that it has not been tampered with. It includes recording how the evidence was collected, transferred, and stored.
Courts evaluate these factors to determine whether electronic evidence can be considered valid and useful in legal proceedings.

10.3 Relevance of Electronic Evidence (Sections 65A & 65B)

Sections 65A and 65B of the Indian Evidence Act, 1872, provide specific guidelines on the relevance and admissibility of electronic records:

1. Section 65A: Provides for the admissibility of electronic records as evidence, acknowledging that digital records have the same legal standing as traditional records if they meet certain criteria.

2. Section 65B: Details the conditions for admissibility:

a. Computer Production: The electronic record must have been produced by a computer during regular business activities.

b. Regular Use: The computer must have been used regularly for the creation and storage of records. This ensures that the records are reliable and were not fabricated.

c. Business Records: The record must be made in the course of ordinary business operations. This includes ensuring that the record was kept as part of routine business activities.

d. Certificate: A certificate must accompany the electronic record, providing details about how the record was created, stored, and maintained. This certificate must be signed by a person in charge of the computer system, affirming that the record meets the criteria specified in Section 65B.

These sections are essential for ensuring that electronic evidence is handled consistently and meets legal standards for admissibility.

10.4 Proof of Electronic Signatures (Section 67A)

Section 67A of the Indian Evidence Act addresses the proof of electronic signatures:

1. Electronic Signature: A digital equivalent of a handwritten signature to authenticate electronic documents. It ensures the identity of the signer and the integrity of the document.

2. Proof Requirements: To prove an electronic signature, one must demonstrate:

a. Affixation: The electronic signature was affixed by the person in question, indicating that they consented to the document's content.

b. Document Integrity: After applying the signature, the document has not been altered. This can be verified using digital signature technology that ensures any changes to the document will invalidate the signature.

c. Authentication: The electronic signature must be authenticated using appropriate cryptographic techniques. This involves verifying that the signature corresponds to the signer's public key and is valid.

Section 67A establishes the legal framework for recognising and validating electronic signatures in legal contexts.

10.5 Verification of Digital Signatures (Section 73A)

Section 73A deals with the verification of digital signatures:

1. Digital Signature: A mathematical scheme used to verify the authenticity and integrity of digital documents. It involves generating a unique signature using the sender's private key, which others can verify using the sender's public key.

2. Verification Process: The process involves:

a. Signature Validation: Using cryptographic algorithms to verify that the digital signature matches the document and corresponds to the sender's public key.

b. Certificate Validation: Checking the digital certificate associated with the signature to ensure it is valid and has not expired or been revoked.

c. Document Integrity: Ensuring the document has not been altered since the signature was applied.

Section 73A ensures that digital signatures are recognised as valid and legally binding when verified according to established procedures.

10.6 Presumptions under Evidence Act (85A, 85B, 85C)

Sections 85A, 85B, and 85C of the Indian Evidence Act establish presumptions related to electronic evidence:

Section 85A: Presumes that electronic records are genuine if produced by the conditions laid out in Section 65B. This presumption simplifies the process of proving the authenticity of electronic documents.

Section 85B: Presumes that electronic signatures and documents signed electronically are valid if they comply with the criteria established for digital signatures. This presumption helps establish the validity of electronic records in legal proceedings.

Section 85C: Presumes that electronic records maintained by a computer are authentic if produced during regular business activities. This presumption is based on the assumption that such records are reliable and kept in the ordinary course of business.

These presumptions facilitate the acceptance of electronic evidence by reducing the burden of proof on the parties presenting the evidence.

10.7 Handling and Preservation of Electronic Evidence

Handling and Preservation of electronic evidence involve several critical steps:
Collection: Using forensic tools and techniques to create exact, bit-for-bit copies of digital evidence to prevent alteration. This process includes securing the original evidence and making duplicate copies for analysis.
Preservation: Ensuring evidence is stored securely to prevent tampering, damage, or loss. This involves using secure storage devices and maintaining controlled access.
Documentation: Keeping detailed records of how evidence was collected, transferred, and stored. This includes recording the chain of custody and any actions taken with the evidence to ensure its integrity.
Integrity Checks: Regularly verifying the integrity of the evidence to ensure it has not been altered. This involves using hash functions to create and check cryptographic hashes of the evidence.
Effective handling and preservation are essential to maintain the credibility and admissibility of electronic evidence in legal proceedings.

10.8 Challenges in Presenting Electronic Evidence in Court

Challenges in presenting electronic evidence include:
Complexity: The technical nature of electronic evidence can be difficult for non-experts, including judges and juries, to understand. This requires a clear and compelling presentation of the evidence.
Authentication: Proving the authenticity of electronic evidence can be challenging, particularly if the evidence has been modified or if the technology used for authentication is flawed.
Chain of Custody: Maintaining and documenting the chain of custody is crucial, but multiple handlers and transfers of the evidence can complicate it.
Privacy Concerns: Electronic evidence handling must balance the need for evidence collection with privacy rights and regulations, such as Data protection laws.
Volatility: Electronic evidence can be volatile and subject to change, which requires prompt and accurate handling to preserve its integrity.
Addressing these challenges is crucial for ensuring electronic evidence is effectively presented and accepted in court.

10.9 International Perspectives on Electronic Evidence

International Perspectives on electronic evidence involve:
Legal Frameworks: Countries have varying laws and standards for handling electronic evidence. For example, the EU's General Data Protection Regulation (GDPR) governs Data privacy and protection, while the US's Federal Rules of Evidence address the admissibility of digital evidence.
Cross-Border Issues: Handling electronic evidence across international borders can be complex due to differences in legal standards and privacy regulations. This often requires global cooperation and agreements.
Standardization: Efforts to standardise practices include international treaties and conventions, such as the Hague Convention on Cybercrime, which aim to facilitate international cooperation and improve the handling of electronic evidence.
Understanding these perspectives is essential for navigating the complexities of cross-border investigations and legal proceedings involving electronic evidence.

10.10 Future Trends in Digital Evidence Law

Future Trends in digital evidence law include:
Technological Advancements: Emerging technologies, such as blockchain and advanced encryption, will impact how evidence is collected, analysed, and protected. New tools and techniques will be developed to address evolving digital environments.
Enhanced Privacy Protections: As privacy concerns grow, there will be an increasing emphasis on balancing evidence collection with individual rights and Data protection regulations.
Artificial Intelligence: AI and machine learning are increasingly prevalent in analysing and managing electronic evidence. These technologies can enhance the efficiency and accuracy of evidence analysis.
Regulatory Changes: Legal frameworks will continue to evolve to address new challenges and technologies. Updates to laws and regulations will address the growing complexity of digital evidence and its role in legal proceedings.

Staying informed about these trends is crucial for adapting legal practices and ensuring effective digital evidence management in the future.

10.11 Glossary

1. Definition of Electronic Evidence

Electronic Evidence: Data or information stored or transmitted in digital form that can be used in legal proceedings. Includes emails, digital documents, system logs, multimedia files, Databases, and metaData.

2. Admissibility of Electronic Evidence

Admissibility: Electronic evidence must be accepted in court, including relevance, reliability, authenticity, and proper chain of custody.

3. Relevance of Electronic Evidence (Sections 65A & 65B)

Section 65A: Part of the Indian Evidence Act that recognises electronic records as valid evidence.

Section 65B: Details the conditions for admissibility of electronic records, including requirements for computer production, regular use, business records, and accompanying certification.

Proof of Electronic Signatures (Section 67A)

Electronic Signature: A digital method for signing electronic documents to authenticate the signer's identity and document integrity.

Proof Requirements: Conditions to prove an electronic signature, including affixation, document integrity, and authentication using cryptographic techniques.

4. Verification of Digital Signatures (Section 73A)

Digital Signature: A cryptographic technique used to validate the authenticity and integrity of digital documents.

Verification Process: This involves validating the signature against the document, checking the digital certificate, and ensuring document integrity.

5. Presumptions under Evidence Act (Sections 85A, 85B, 85C)

Section 85A: Presumption that electronic records are genuine if produced according to Section 65B.

Section 85B: Presumption that electronic signatures and documents signed electronically are valid if they meet legal criteria.

Section 85C: Presumption that electronic records maintained by a computer are authentic if produced during regular business activities.

6. Handling and Preservation of Electronic Evidence

Collection: Obtaining exact copies of digital evidence to ensure it remains unaltered.

Preservation: Storing evidence securely to prevent tampering or loss, including controlled access and secure storage devices.

Documentation: Recording the chain of custody and actions taken with the evidence to maintain integrity.

Integrity Checks: Verifying evidence remains unaltered using cryptographic hash functions.

7. Challenges in Presenting Electronic Evidence in Court

Complexity: The technical nature of electronic evidence may be difficult for non-experts to understand.

Authentication: Proving evidence is authentic can be challenging if there are issues with technology or modifications.

Chain of Custody: Maintaining and documenting evidence handling is critical but complex.

Privacy Concerns: Balancing evidence collection with privacy rights and Data protection laws.

Volatility: Electronic evidence can change over time, requiring prompt and accurate handling.

8. International Perspectives on Electronic Evidence

Legal Frameworks: Varied laws and standards across countries for handling electronic evidence.

Cross-Border Issues: Challenges in managing evidence across international borders due to different legal and privacy regulations.

Standardization: Efforts to create international agreements and standards, such as the Hague Convention on Cybercrime, to facilitate cross-border cooperation.

9. Future Trends in Digital Evidence Law

Technological Advancements: Impact of emerging technologies like blockchain and advanced encryption on evidence collection and protection.

Enhanced Privacy Protections: Growing focus on privacy and Data protection in evidence collection.

Artificial Intelligence: Use of AI and machine learning to improve the analysis and management of electronic evidence.

Regulatory Changes: Evolving legal frameworks to address new challenges and technologies in digital evidence management.

10.12 Summary

1. Definition of Electronic Evidence

Electronic evidence includes Data or information stored or transmitted digitally that is used in legal proceedings. It encompasses emails, digital documents, system logs, multimedia files, Databases, and metaData. Proper understanding and management of these various forms of digital evidence are crucial for legal processes.

2. Admissibility of Electronic Evidence

For electronic evidence to be admissible in court, it must be relevant to the case, reliable, authentic, and properly handled. This includes ensuring the evidence is directly related to the case, obtained through legitimate means, and preserved with a documented chain of custody. The court evaluates these criteria to determine the evidence's acceptance.

3. Relevance of Electronic Evidence (Sections 65A & 65B)

Sections 65A and 65B of the Indian Evidence Act provide guidelines for the relevance and admissibility of electronic records. Section 65A acknowledges electronic records as valid evidence. In contrast, Section 65B outlines the conditions for their admissibility, including requirements for computer production, regular use, business records, and certification by the person in charge of the computer system.

4. Proof of Electronic Signatures (Section 67A)

Section 67A addresses the proof of electronic signatures, which are digital equivalents of handwritten signatures used to authenticate electronic documents. Proof requirements include demonstrating that the person in question applied the signature, that the document has not been altered, and that the signature is authenticated through cryptographic techniques.

5. Verification of Digital Signatures (Section 73A)

Section 73A covers the verification of digital signatures, which involves confirming the authenticity and integrity of digital documents. The verification process includes validating the signature against the document, checking the associated digital certificate, and ensuring that the document has not been altered since the signature was applied.

6. Presumptions under Evidence Act (Sections 85A, 85B, 85C)

Sections 85A, 85B, and 85C establish presumptions regarding electronic evidence. Section 85A presumes that electronic records are genuine if they comply with Section 65B. Section 85B presumes the validity of electronic signatures and documents signed electronically. Section 85C presumes that electronic records maintained by a computer are authentic if they are produced during regular business activities.

7. Handling and Preservation of Electronic Evidence

Handling and preserving electronic evidence involves collecting exact copies of digital evidence, securing its storage to prevent tampering, documenting the chain of custody, and conducting integrity checks using cryptographic hash functions. These practices ensure that the evidence remains intact and admissible in court.

8. Challenges in Presenting Electronic Evidence in Court

Presenting electronic evidence in court involves overcoming challenges such as the technical complexity of the evidence, proving authenticity, maintaining the chain of custody, addressing privacy concerns, and managing evidence volatility. Effective presentation requires clear explanation and robust handling procedures.

9. International Perspectives on Electronic Evidence

International perspectives on electronic evidence include varying legal frameworks across countries, challenges in managing evidence across borders, and efforts to standardise practices through international treaties and agreements like the Hague Convention on Cybercrime. These factors influence how electronic evidence is handled globally.

10.13 Previous Year Solved Questions

Ques. How do the legal principles and statutory provisions under Indian law ensure the effective handling and admissibility of electronic evidence in cybercrime cases, and what are the critical challenges faced in presenting such evidence in court? Discuss the relevant sections of the Indian Evidence Act and their implications, including the role of electronic signatures, digital signatures, and the handling of electronic records. (Udaipur University, 2022 MCA)

Ans. In the realm of cybercrime investigations, the handling and admissibility of electronic evidence are governed by several legal principles and statutory provisions under Indian law, primarily found in the Indian Evidence Act of 1872. These provisions aim to ensure that electronic evidence is treated with the same level of credibility and reliability as traditional evidence, provided it meets certain criteria.

1. Legal Framework for Electronic Evidence:

The Indian Evidence Act has been updated to address the challenges posed by electronic evidence. The relevant sections include:

Section 65A: This section acknowledges the validity of electronic records as evidence in legal proceedings, thereby establishing that electronic evidence is on par with physical records. It allows electronic documents to be admissible if they meet the criteria set out in Section 65B.
Section 65B: Details the conditions for the admissibility of electronic records. It requires that the electronic record be produced by a computer in the regular course of business, maintained regularly, and accompanied by a certificate affirming these conditions. This section ensures that electronic records are reliable and authentic by requiring detailed certification of their origin and maintenance.
Section 67A: Addresses the proof of electronic signatures used to authenticate electronic documents. This section mandates that electronic signatures must be verified to prove their authenticity, ensuring that the signature is genuinely affixed by the purported signatory and that the document remains unaltered.
Section 73A: Focuses on the verification of digital signatures. It provides a framework for validating digital signatures through cryptographic techniques, ensuring that the signature corresponds to the signer's public key and maintains the document's integrity.
Sections 85A, 85B, and 85C: These sections establish presumptions regarding the authenticity of electronic records and signatures. Section 85A presumes that electronic records are genuine if they comply with Section 65B. Section 85B presumes the validity of electronic signatures, while Section 85C presumes that electronic records maintained in regular business activities are authentic.

2. Key Challenges in Presenting Electronic Evidence:

Despite these statutory provisions, presenting electronic evidence in court involves several challenges:
Complexity: The technical nature of electronic evidence can be difficult for judges, juries, and legal professionals to understand. This complexity requires a clear and compelling presentation of evidence, often necessitating expert testimony to explain technical aspects.
Authentication: Proving the authenticity of electronic evidence is challenging, particularly if the evidence has been modified or if the technology used for authentication is flawed. This requires rigorous verification processes and demonstrating that the evidence has not been tampered with.
Chain of Custody: Maintaining a documented chain of custody is crucial for ensuring the integrity of electronic evidence. This involves recording each person who handles the evidence and ensuring it is stored securely. Any lapses in the chain of custody can undermine the evidence's credibility.
Privacy Concerns: Collecting and presenting electronic evidence must balance the need for evidence with privacy rights and Data protection laws. Ensuring compliance with privacy regulations while collecting evidence is a significant challenge.
Volatility: Electronic evidence can be volatile and subject to change, which requires prompt and accurate handling to preserve its integrity. This volatility necessitates the use of secure storage solutions and regular integrity checks.

3. Implications and Future Considerations:

The legal framework provided by the Indian Evidence Act aims to standardise the treatment of electronic evidence, making it a reliable and admissible form of evidence in court. However, new challenges and trends in digital evidence law will emerge as technology evolves. Future considerations include technological advancements like blockchain and artificial intelligence, impacting how evidence is collected, analysed, and protected. Additionally, evolving privacy protections and regulatory changes will further shape the landscape of electronic evidence handling.
In conclusion, while the Indian Evidence Act provides a robust framework for the admissibility and handling of electronic evidence, the effectiveness of these provisions depends on overcoming the inherent challenges associated with digital evidence. Ensuring proper authentication, maintaining the chain of custody, and addressing privacy concerns are critical for successfully presenting electronic evidence in court.

Exercises

Exercise 1 – Multiple Choice Questions

1. Which section of the Indian Evidence Act recognizes electronic records as valid evidence?
a) Section 65A
b) Section 67A
c) Section 85A
d) Section 73A

2. What is the main purpose of a digital signature?
a) To enhance document formatting

b) To verify the authenticity and integrity of digital documents
c) To encrypt Data
d) To store Data securely

Exercise 2 – True/False
1. Section 65B outlines the conditions for the admissibility of electronic records.
2. Electronic evidence includes only multimedia files and Databases.

Exercise 3 – Fill in the blanks
1. For electronic evidence to be admissible in court, it must be relevant, reliable, authentic, and properly __________. (chain of custody / evidence handling)
2. The process of validating a digital signature involves checking the associated __________ and ensuring document integrity. (certificate / metaData)

Exercise 4- Fill in the blanks with two options
1. Section 67A deals with the proof of __________ or __________ signatures. (electronic / digital)
2. Handling electronic evidence involves __________ exact copies and __________ the chain of custody. (collecting / preserving / destroying / securing)

Exercise 5- Rearrange the sentence
1. (handling / chain of custody / maintaining / documenting / electronic evidence)
2. (digital signature / verifying / involves / cryptographic techniques / the use of)

Exercise 6- Choose the Odd One Out
1. Electronic Evidence / Chain of Custody / MetaData / Email
2. Section 67A / Section 85A / Section 73A / Indian Penal Code

Exercise 7- Jumble words
1. OCEDSP / ANLEOCRTIC / TCEIEEVD
2. TROUCAHNICIT / DNIGIOLRNTI / ESTIDGNEPOT

Exercise 8- Match case
1. Electronic Evidence
2. Chain of Custody
3. Section 67A
4. Section 65A

a) Proves authenticity of signatures
b) Section 65A
c) Preserving evidence
d) Data or information in digital form

Exercise 9- Assertion – Reason
1. Assertion: Section 65B of the Indian Evidence Act outlines the conditions for admissibility of electronic records.
Reason: It specifies requirements for computer production, regular use, and business records.
a) Both Assertion and Reason are correct and Reason is the correct explanation for Assertion.
b) Both Assertion and Reason are correct but Reason is not the correct explanation for Assertion.
c) Assertion is correct but Reason is incorrect.
d) Assertion is incorrect but Reason is correct.
2. Assertion: Electronic evidence must be handled and preserved with proper documentation.
Reason: This ensures that the evidence remains intact and admissible in court.
a) Both Assertion and Reason are correct and Reason is the correct explanation for Assertion.
b) Both Assertion and Reason are correct but Reason is not the correct explanation for Assertion.
c) Assertion is correct but Reason is incorrect.
d) Assertion is incorrect but Reason is correct.

Exercise 10- Read the questions given below and find the appropriate word in the grid provided.
Questions:

1. The principle that requires electronic evidence to be relevant, reliable, authentic, and properly handled to be accepted in court is known as ___________.
2. The sections of the Indian Evidence Act that provide guidelines for the admissibility of electronic records, including requirements for computer production and certification, are ___________ and ___________.

Grid:

A	I	J	B	J	Q	N	L	H	W	A	C
D	E	R	A	B	I	L	I	T	B	D	Y
M	O	P	V	N	M	P	Y	H	E	S	E
I	N	E	S	S	N	O	U	R	E	D	R
S	E	C	T	I	O	N	6	5	A	T	G
S	E	C	T	I	O	N	6	5	B	G	A
I	T	R	C	A	G	W	M	G	E	F	L
B	W	E	R	T	Y	U	I	O	P	L	K
I	A	S	D	F	G	H	J	K	L	O	I
L	Z	X	C	V	B	N	A	S	D	F	G
I	M	E	B	E	E	R	T	A	C	K	E
T	Y	U	O	R	A	C	E	A	T	C	T
Y	E	S	S	I	O	N	T	E	S	T	G

Exercise 11- One- word

1. What is the term for Data or information stored or transmitted digitally used in legal proceedings?
2. What is the process of validating the authenticity and integrity of digital documents called?

Exercise 12- Small Answers

1. Explain the significance of Section 65B in the context of electronic evidence.
2. What are the main challenges in presenting electronic evidence in court?

Exercise 13- Long Answers

1. Discuss the importance of handling and preservation of electronic evidence and the best practices involved.
2. Describe the provisions of the Indian Evidence Act that pertain to electronic signatures and their verification.

Exercise 14- Previous Year Unsolved Questions

1. Discuss the role of Section 65B in the admissibility of electronic evidence in Indian courts. How does it ensure that electronic records are accepted as valid evidence? (Udaipur University, December 2022, MCA)
2. Explain the process and significance of verifying digital signatures under Section 73A of the Indian Evidence Act. What steps are involved in this verification process? (Udaipur University, December 2022, MCA)
3. Discuss security issues in Cyberspace. (IGNOU, December 2022, MCA)
4. Write a note on Cyber Forensics (IGNOU, December 2022, MCA)
5. Give an overview of Cyberspace regulation in India. (IGNOU, December 2022, MCA)
6. Discuss the six principles of Security Management. (IGNOU, December 2022, MCA)

Answers

Exercise 1- 1. d) All of the above 2. b) Section 67A
Exercise 2- 1. True, 2. True
Exercise 3- 1. digital, 2. authentic
Exercise 4- 1. Section 65A, 2. Digital signatures
Exercise 5- 1. Maintain and document the chain of custody to ensure the integrity of the evidence. 2. Section 65A provides guidelines for the admissibility of electronic records.
Exercise 6- 1. Cyber Stalking, 2. Section 73A

Exercise 7- 1. Electronic evidence includes digital emails. 2. Admissibility of evidence must include relevance and reliability.
Exercise 8- 1 – c, 2 - a 3, - b, 4 - d
Exercise 9- 1. Both Assertion and Reason are correct, and the Reason correctly explains the Assertion. 2. Both Assertion and Reason are correct, and the Reason correctly explains the Assertion.
Exercise 10- 1. ADMISSIBILITY, 2. SECTION 65A and SECTION 65B

A	I	J	B	J	Q	N	L	H	W	A	C
D	E	R	A	B	I	L	I	T	B	D	Y
M	O	P	V	N	M	P	Y	H	E	S	E
I	N	E	S	S	N	O	U	R	E	D	R
S	E	C	T	I	O	N	6	5	A	T	G
S	E	C	T	I	O	N	6	5	B	G	A
I	T	R	C	A	G	W	M	G	E	F	L
B	W	E	R	T	Y	U	I	O	P	L	K
I	A	S	D	F	G	H	J	K	L	O	I
L	Z	X	C	V	B	N	A	S	D	F	G
I	M	E	B	E	E	R	T	A	C	K	E
T	Y	U	O	R	A	C	E	A	T	C	T
Y	E	S	S	I	O	N	T	E	S	T	G

Exercise 11- 1. Verification, 2. Electronic Signature

Test Paper

Chapter-10

Law of Evidence in Cyber Crimes

Time Duration: 30 **Maximum Marks: 25**

General Instructions:

1. The question paper consists of 12 questions and is divided into four sections, A, B, C and D.
2. All questions are compulsory.
3. Section A comprises MCQs, Fill in the blanks and True or False carrying one marks each.
4. Section B comprises VSAQs(very short answers questions) carrying two marks each.
5. Section C comprises SAQs(short questions) carrying four marks each.
6. Section D comprises long questions carrying five marks each.

SECTION-A

I. Multiple choice questions: **(1*2=2)**

1. What is required to prove the admissibility of electronic evidence in court?
a) Relevance
b) Reliability
c) Authenticity
d) All of the above

2. Which section of the Indian Evidence Act addresses the presumption that electronic records are genuine?
a) Section 65A
b) Section 85A
c) Section 67A
d) Section 73A

II. Fill in the blanks: **(1*2=2)**

1. Section 67A addresses the proof of __________ signatures.
2. To maintain the integrity of electronic evidence, it is crucial to document the __________ of custody.

III. True or False: **(1*2=2)**

1. Section 65B outlines the conditions for the admissibility of electronic records.
2. Digital signatures are used to validate the authenticity of physical documents.

SECTION-B

IV. Very Short answers type questions-I **(2*3=6)**

1. What does Section 65A of the Indian Evidence Act pertain to?
2. Describe the verification process for digital signatures.
3. What are the challenges in presenting electronic evidence in court?

SECTION-C

V. Short answers type questions-II **(4*2=8)**

1. Explain the requirements for the admissibility of electronic evidence under Section 65B.
2. Discuss the role of Section 85B in the presumption of electronic signatures and documents.

SECTION-D

VI. Long answers type questions **(5*1=5)**

1. Describe the handling and preservation processes for electronic evidence. How do these processes ensure that evidence remains intact and admissible in court?

ONLINE RESOURCES

Practice Paper
Link: https://forms.gle/Sh4qxuo23nJxSFRN9
QR Code:

YouTube Video Playlist Link
Link: https://www.youtube.com/playlist?list=PLzlh_31VWEFpC-iHwOgn6mTWCpOepn0Oe
QR Code:

Chapter 11 - Viva Voce

Question 1. What is cyberspace?
Answer: Cyberspace is the virtual environment where digital communication occurs, encompassing the internet and various networks.
Question 2. How does the Internet of Things (IoT) enhance connectivity?
Answer: IoT enhances connectivity by allowing everyday objects to connect to the internet, enabling them to collect and exchange Data.
Question 3. Define cybercrime.
Answer: Cybercrime is any criminal activity conducted through computers or the internet, involving actions such as Data theft, hacking, or fraud.
Question 4. What are the common types of cyber crimes?
Answer: Common types of cyber crimes include phishing, malware distribution, identity theft, and denial of service attacks.
Question 5. Who are considered cyber criminals?
Answer: Cyber criminals are individuals or groups who use computers and the internet to commit illegal activities, including fraud, theft, and other malicious acts.
Question 6. What motivates individuals to engage in cybercrime?
Answer: Motivations for cybercrime can include financial gain, political activism, personal revenge, or the challenge of overcoming security measures.
Question 7. What are the major cyber security threats?
Answer: Major cyber security threats include malware, ransomware, phishing attacks, and insider threats.
Question 8. How can cyber threats impact organisations?
Answer: Cyber threats can lead to financial losses, damage to reputation, operational disruptions, and the compromise of sensitive information.
Question 9. What is the purpose of cyber laws?
Answer: Cyber laws regulate online behaviour, protect digital information, and provide legal frameworks for addressing and prosecuting cyber crimes.
Question 10. Name one critical cyber law in your region.
Answer: One critical cyber law is the Information Technology Act in India, which addresses various aspects of cybercrime and electronic commerce.
Question 11. What is the role of law enforcement in cyber security?
Answer: Law enforcement plays a role in investigating cyber crimes, enforcing cyber laws, and coordinating with other agencies to address cyber threats.
Question 12. How do law enforcement agencies respond to cyber crimes?
Answer: Law enforcement agencies respond by conducting investigations, gathering and analysing digital evidence, prosecuting offenders, and collaborating with international organisations.
Question 13. Define "phishing."
Answer: Phishing is a fraudulent attempt to acquire sensitive information by pretending to be a trustworthy entity in electronic communications.
Question 14. What is meant by "malware"?
Answer: Malware refers to malicious software designed to disrupt, damage, or gain unauthorised access to computer systems.
Question 15. What are the key takeaways from the chapter?
Answer: Key takeaways include understanding the scope of cyber security, the types of threats, and the legal framework for managing cyber incidents.
Question 16. How does this chapter contribute to understanding cyber security?
Answer: The chapter provides foundational knowledge on cyber security concepts, threats, and the legal aspects of managing cyber incidents.
Question 17. What is a typical exam question related to cyber crimes?
Answer: A typical exam question might involve defining different types of cyber crimes and their impacts on individuals and organisations.
Question 18. How can reviewing the previous year's questions help in exam preparation?
Answer: Reviewing the previous year's questions helps in understanding the exam format, identifying essential topics, and practising answers.

Question 19. What is the significance of network security in cyber protection?
Answer: Network security is crucial for protecting Data and resources from unauthorised access, misuse, and attacks, ensuring the integrity and confidentiality of information.
Question 20. What are MITM (Man-In-The-Middle) attacks?
Answer: MITM attacks involve an attacker intercepting and potentially altering the communication between two parties without their knowledge.
Question 21. How does ARP spoofing affect network security?
Answer: ARP spoofing involves falsifying ARP messages to associate the attacker's MAC address with the IP address of another device, potentially leading to Data interception or disruption.
Question 22. What is IP spoofing?
Answer: IP spoofing is the creation of IP packets with a forged source address to deceive network devices into accepting them as legitimate.
Question 23. Define DNS attacks.
Answer: DNS attacks involve exploiting vulnerabilities in the Domain Name System to redirect users to malicious sites or disrupt network services.
Question 24. What is SYN flooding?
Answer: SYN flooding is a type of DoS attack where the attacker sends a flood of SYN requests to overwhelm a target's resources and prevent legitimate connections.
Question 25. Explain DoS and DDoS attacks.
Answer: DoS (Denial of Service) attacks aim to disrupt a service by overwhelming it with traffic, while DDoS (Distributed Denial of Service) attacks use multiple systems to amplify the attack.
Question 26. Why is network penetration testing important?
Answer: Network penetration testing is essential to identify and address vulnerabilities in a network before malicious attackers can exploit them.
Question 27. What is the role of firewalls in network security?
Answer: Firewalls monitor and control incoming and outgoing network traffic based on predetermined security rules to prevent unauthorised access.
Question 28. How do IDS/IPS systems enhance network security?
Answer: IDS (Intrusion Detection Systems) and IPS (Intrusion Prevention Systems) detect and respond to potential security breaches by monitoring network traffic and blocking malicious activities.
Question 29. What are the key security protocols for wireless networks?
Answer: Key security protocols for wireless networks include WPA2 (Wi-Fi Protected Access II) and WPA3, which provide encryption and authentication to secure wireless communications.
Question 30. How do cookies contribute to web application security?
Answer: Cookies store session information and user preferences, essential for securely managing authentication and user sessions.
Question 31. What are the OWASP Top 10 Flaws?
Answer: The OWASP Top 10 Flaws list the most critical web application security risks, including issues like injection attacks, broken authentication, and sensitive Data exposure.
Question 32. Why is input validation crucial for web security?
Answer: Input validation is crucial to prevent attackers from injecting malicious Data that could compromise the web application's security.
Question 33. What is vulnerability assessment?
Answer: Vulnerability assessment identifies and evaluates security weaknesses in a system to address potential risks.
Question 34. How does defensive software architecture improve security?
Answer: Defensive software architecture involves designing software to anticipate and mitigate security threats, enhancing overall protection.
Question 35. What is the purpose of responsible disclosure programs?
Answer: Responsible disclosure programs encourage security researchers to report vulnerabilities to organisations so they can be addressed before being publicly disclosed.

ONLINE RESOURCES

Practice Paper
Link: https://forms.gle/AFwegofFLc31qNFm7

QR Code:

YouTube Video Playlist Link

Link: https://www.youtube.com/playlist?list=PLzlh_31VWEFpXsrMQUJVHrYTAig5ZOjSk

QR Code:

Chapter 12 - Project And Case Study

12.1 Project Title: Development and Implementation of a Cyber Security Framework for E-Commerce

Objective: Create a robust cyber security framework for an e-commerce platform, addressing network security, web application security, malware analysis, and legal compliance to protect against cyber threats and ensure secure transactions.

Project Components

1. Overview of Cyber Security Needs

Description: Conduct an initial assessment of the e-commerce platform's cyber security posture. Identify key vulnerabilities and areas for improvement.

Key Areas: Cyberspace, IoT implications, and existing cyber threats.

2. Network Security Enhancement

Description: Develop and implement strategies to secure the network infrastructure from various attack vectors.

Actions: Deploy firewalls, IDS/IPS systems, and secure wireless protocols. Mitigate risks associated with MITM attacks, ARP spoofing, and DDoS attacks.

3. Web Application Security Improvements

Description: Implement measures to protect web applications from common vulnerabilities.

Actions: Apply OWASP best practices, enhance input validation, and improve defensive software architecture. Conduct vulnerability assessments and penetration testing.

4. Malware Detection and Response

Description: Establish procedures for detecting, analysing, and responding to malware threats.

Actions: Use static and dynamic techniques, conduct behavioural analysis, and employ sandboxing technologies for thorough malware examination.

5. Cyber Crime Investigation Protocols

Description: Develop protocols for investigating cyber crimes and managing digital evidence.

Actions: Set up procedures for digital evidence collection, chain of custody maintenance, and incident reporting. Ensure alignment with international cooperation standards.

12.2 Case Study: Secure E-Commerce Platform

Scenario: An e-commerce platform has been experiencing security breaches, including network attacks and web application vulnerabilities. The company seeks a comprehensive security solution to enhance protection, ensure compliance, and improve overall security posture.

Tasks:

1. Initial Assessment

Objective: Identify current security weaknesses and areas needing improvement.

Outcome: Report on existing vulnerabilities and threats.

2. Network Security Upgrades

Objective: Enhance protection against network-based attacks.

Outcome: Implemented firewalls, intrusion detection systems, and secured network protocols.

3. Web Application Security

Objective: Protect web applications from common flaws and vulnerabilities.

Outcome: Applied OWASP security practices and conducted vulnerability testing.

4. Malware Analysis Implementation

Objective: Detect and mitigate malware threats effectively.

Outcome: Established procedures for malware analysis and response.

5. Cyber Crime Investigation Framework

Objective: Develop protocols for investigating and managing cyber crimes.

Outcome: Implemented digital evidence handling procedures and incident reporting standards.

6. Legal and Compliance Review

Objective: Ensure all security measures comply with legal and ethical standards.

Outcome: Updated policies to align with cyber laws and privacy regulations.

Chapter 13 - Sample Exam Paper

General Instructions:
Time Allowed: 3 Hours
Maximum Marks: 100
Answer all the questions.
Marks are indicated against each question.

SECTION-A

I. Multiple Choice Questions **(2*5=20 Marks)**

1. Which of the following is considered a cybercrime?
a) Online shopping
b) Identity theft
c) Blogging
d) Sending email

2. The main objective of a DoS (Denial of Service) attack is to:
a) Gain unauthorized access to Data
b) Overload the system and deny service to legitimate users
c) Alter system settings
d) Install malware on a system

3. ARP Spoofing is an attack related to:
a) Application security
b) DNS servers
c) Network traffic interception
d) Web authentication

4. The OWASP Top 10 refers to:
a) The most common network security protocols
b) The top 10 web application security flaws
c) A set of malware analysis techniques
d) Common types of firewalls used in network security

5. Which section of the IT Act 2000 deals with digital signatures?
a) Section 65A
b) Section 67A
c) Section 73A
d) Section 85A

II. Fill in the Blanks **(2*5=20 Marks)**

1. __________ is a technique where the attacker intercepts and relays messages between two parties who believe they are directly communicating with each other.
2. The acronym DDoS stands for __________.
3. The Common Vulnerability Scoring System (CVSS) is used to __________ vulnerabilities.
4. In cyber forensics, the process of maintaining the integrity of evidence from collection to presentation in court is called __________.
5. The admissibility of electronic evidence is defined under Section __________ of the Indian Evidence Act.

SECTION-B

III. Very Short Answer Type Questions-I **(4*5=20 Marks)**

1. Define cybercrime and provide two examples of cybercrimes.
2. Explain the purpose of firewalls in network security.
3. What are the key components of cyber forensics?
4. How does two-factor authentication improve security?
5. What is the significance of digital evidence in cybercrime investigations?

SECTION-C

IV. Short Answer Type Questions-II **(6*5=30 Marks)**

1. Explain the difference between DoS and DDoS attacks.
2. Describe the concept of vulnerability management and discuss its importance in cybersecurity.
3. What is session management in web applications, and why is it critical to security?
4. Discuss the legal and ethical issues surrounding cybersecurity and the role of cyber laws in addressing these issues.
5. How do international cooperation and cybercrime investigations work together in addressing global cyber threats?

SECTION-D

V. Long Answer Type Questions **(10*3=30 Marks)**

1. Discuss the common types of network attacks, including MITM, ARP spoofing, and DNS attacks. How can organisations safeguard themselves against these attacks using firewalls, IDS/IPS, and other techniques?
2. Describe the cybercrime investigation process from evidence collection to presentation in court. What role does digital forensics play in ensuring the success of such investigations, and what challenges exist in presenting electronic evidence?
3. Discuss the importance of API testing in web penetration testing and outline the critical steps involved in performing effective API security testing.

In this book

In a world where the digital and physical realms are increasingly intertwined, cybersecurity has emerged as one of the most critical challenges of our time. Every click, every keystroke, and every online interaction carries with it the potential for risk, making the need for robust security measures more important than ever before.

This book is born out of the recognition that cybersecurity is not just a technical field reserved for experts—it is a discipline that touches every aspect of modern life. From individuals managing their personal Data to organizations protecting sensitive information, and governments safeguarding national security, cybersecurity is a shared responsibility that demands awareness, understanding, and proactive measures.

Throughout this book, we will explore the foundational concepts of cybersecurity, providing readers with a solid

In an age where cyber threats are constantly evolving, staying informed is not just an option—it is a necessity. The aim of this book is to equip you with the knowledge and tools you need to navigate the complex world of cybersecurity with confidence. As you read, you will gain insights into real-world scenarios, learn practical skills, and develop a mindset that is both defensive and proactive.

YouTube Videos Playlists for all Chapters

Chapter 1
Link: https://www.youtube.com/playlist?list=PLzlh_31VWEFqw6Ah-eeBO1Lwh5Qmq20K_
QR Code:

Chapter 2
Link: **https://www.youtube.com/playlist?list=PLzlh_31VWEFqeuC6U2ueE1kVARD8WTeKJ**
QR Code:

Chapter 3
Link: https://www.youtube.com/playlist?list=PLzlh_31VWEFoQmknN6oEeZarlNzsUELrh
QR Code:

Chapter 4
Link: https://www.youtube.com/playlist?list=PLzlh_31VWEFpGMEC_dHVJPS7agg6h8cu5
QR Code:

Chapter 5
Link: https://www.youtube.com/playlist?list=PLzlh_31VWEFpQ1P6Rw75QdPfiNpoceI17
QR Code:

Chapter 6
Link: https://www.youtube.com/playlist?list=PLzlh_31VWEFqiHFI-CMpCxfkd5OTd5Mto
QR Code:

Chapter 7
Link: https://www.youtube.com/playlist?list=PLzlh_31VWEFogPis57wcuY8zrKcVLgpBb
QR Code:

Chapter 8
Link: https://www.youtube.com/playlist?list=PLzlh_31VWEFphqGbLIapdVFOs1oxnmIAs
QR Code:

Chapter 9
Link: https://www.youtube.com/playlist?list=PLzlh_31VWEFp4fLLNYOxy3R92HV0elpk7
QR Code:

Chapter 10
Link: https://www.youtube.com/playlist?list=PLzlh_31VWEFpC-iHwOgn6mTWCpOepn0Oe
QR Code:

Chapter 11
Link: https://www.youtube.com/playlist?list=PLzlh_31VWEFpXsrMQUJVHrYTAig5ZOjSk
QR Code:

© Author and Publisher 2024